Marxism and Workers' Self-Management

Recent Titles in
Contributions in Economics and Economic History

Nuclear Power Goes On-Line: A History of Shippingport
William Beaver

The Impact of the Federal Budget Process on National Forest Planning
V. Alaric Sample

American Management and British Labor: A Comparative Study of the Cotton
Spinning Industry
Isaac Cohen

Monopoly Capital Theory: Hilferding and Twentieth-Century Capitalism
Jonas Zoninsein

Korean Economic Development
Jene K. Kwon, editor

From Industry to Arms: The Political Economy of High Technology
Anthony DiFilippo

Semiperipheral States in the World-Economy
William G. Martin, editor

The Econometrics of Disequilibrium Models
V. K. Srivastava and B. Bhaskara Rao

Perspectives on an Economic Future: Forms, Reforms, and Evaluations
Shripad G. Pendse, editor

Electricity in the American Economy: Agent of Technological Progress
*Sam H. Schurr, Calvin C. Burwell, Warren D. Devine, Jr., and Sidney
Sonenblum*

The Great Myths of 1929 and the Lessons to Be Learned
Harold Bierman, Jr.

Arab Nationalism, Oil, and the Political Economy of Dependency
Abbas Alnasrawi

The Rise of a New World Economic Power: Postwar Taiwan
Y. Dolly Hwang

MARXISM and WORKERS' SELF-MANAGEMENT

THE ESSENTIAL TENSION

David L. Prychitko

Contributions in Economics and Economic History, Number 123

GREENWOOD PRESS
New York
Westport, Connecticut
London

Library of Congress Cataloging-in-Publication Data

Prychitko, David L.
  Marxism and workers' self-management : the essential tension /
David L. Prychitko.
      p. cm.—(Contributions in economics and economic history,
  ISSN 0084–9235 ; no. 123)
    Includes bibliographical references (p.   ) and index.
    ISBN 0-313-27854-7 (alk. paper)
    1. Industrial management—Employee participation. 2. Central
planning. 3. Socialism—Yugoslavia. 4. Marx, Karl, 1818–1883.
I. Title. II. Series.
  HD5650.P66   1991
  338.6—dc20   91-9152

British Library Cataloguing in Publication Data is available.

Library of Congress Catalog Card Number: 91-9152
ISBN: 0-313-27854-7
ISSN: 0084-9235

First published in 1991

Greenwood Press, 88 Post Road West, Westport, CT 06881
An imprint of Greenwood Publishing Group, Inc.

Printed in the United States of America

The paper used in this book complies with the
Permanent Paper Standard issued by the National
Information Standards Organization (Z39.48–1984).

10 9 8 7 6 5 4 3 2 1

Copyright Acknowledgments
The author and publisher gratefully acknowledge the following sources for granting
permission to reprint:

Extracts from Karl Marx, *Critique of Hegel's "Philosophy of Right."* New York:
Cambridge University Press, 1970.

Extracts from Branko Horvat, *The Political Economy of Socialism: A Marxist Social
Theory.* Armonk, N.Y.: M.E. Sharpe, Inc., 1982. Permission granted courtesy of
M.E. Sharpe and Branko Horvat.

For Julie

Contents

14/2080

Preface

This book is in no small part the product of generous encouragement and support from my family, friends, and the broader scholarly community. My first debt is owed to my father, Harry, and my late mother, Joanne, who instilled in me the love of learning, the courage of conviction, and the importance of pursuing my interests. Indeed, my family always supported my frequently changing ambitions, from my boyhood thoughts of being a ditch-digger, to my later goals of becoming a writer, naturalist, water scientist, and eventually an academic economist. My sister Maria has been one of my biggest promoters (and probably would have been even had I pursued my boyhood ambition), while my in-laws, Ken and Sonja Johnson, have cheerfully provided me and my wife love and support.

My interest in economics and social theory stems from the exceptional teaching of my undergraduate professors in the department of economics at Northern Michigan University. Howard R. Swaine, in particular, sparked my interest in the socialist calculation debate and the broader questions of comparative political economy, and strongly supported my decision to pursue a Ph.D. at George Mason University, to which I am also grateful. The faculty and graduate students in the department of economics at George Mason University gave me a tremendous intellectual boost, and the Center for the Study of Market Processes, directed by Jack High, provided a warm and exciting atmosphere for its students. Colleen Morretta went far beyond her role as the Center's executive assistant to help me through the many technical entanglements on the road to my doctorate.

Earlier versions of this book were read by Michael Alexeev, Tom R. Burns, Jack High, Don Lavoie, Karen I. Vaughn, and an anonymous reader. Their comments and criticisms greatly improved the project. Don Lavoie's interdisciplinary approach to comparative political economy has been an invaluable inspiration to me. A mentor, colleague, and friend, Don improved this book enormously as he was at once my strongest critic and supporter, and I consider myself very fortunate to have had his input and advice throughout the entire development of this project. I also thank Peter J. Boettke, Steven Horwitz, Jeremy Shearmur, and Ruby J. Shields for their detailed comments and research leads on various parts of this book. Pete and Steve made it all worthwhile.

Several institutions provided generous financial support since the inception of this project: the Center for the Study of Market Processes, the Humane Studies Foundation, and the Earhart Foundation. A fellowship awarded by the Gilder Foundation provided me the invaluable opportunity to visit as a Junior Fellow at the Program on Participation and Labor-Managed Systems directed by Jaroslav Vanek at Cornell University. My many warm conversations with Professor Vanek about the contemporary cooperative movement has shaken free many old, insupportable biases, and has surely strengthened this present work. The Gilder Fellowship, along with a Fulbright grant awarded by the Institute of International Education, afforded me the opportunity to conduct research at the Philosophical Faculty of the University of Zagreb and to participate in the seminars "Self-management in Future Socialism and Capitalism," "Anarchism: Community and Utopia," and "Philosophy and Social Science: 'The End of Utopia'?" at the Inter-University Centre for Postgraduate Studies in Dubrovnik, Yugoslavia, during the spring of 1989. I thank my sponsor Duško Sekulić, the Dubrovnik seminar participants, and my newly found Yugoslav friends for their discussions and insights.

SUNY-Oswego provided a congenial atmosphere and support for the final preparation of the manuscript, and Becky Truax's secretarial support helped me through many tedious revisions. I also thank Cynthia Harris, my editor at Greenwood, for her encouragement in seeing the manuscript into its present form.

Finally, my wife Julie. Her unbounded love and untiring support has made me one very lucky person. I dedicate this book to Julie, with my deepest love, respect, and gratitude.

Introduction

The return to the real Marx as against the Marx...distorted by right wing social democrats and Stalinists, was the goal of the Yugoslav School of Marxist philosophy.

Mihailo Marković (1974)

Our point...is not that dictatorship must inevitably extirpate freedom but rather that planning leads to dictatorship because dictatorship is the most effective instrument of coercion and the enforcement of ideals and, as such, essential if central planning on a large scale is to be possible. The clash between planning and democracy arises simply from the fact that the latter is an obstacle to the suppression of freedom which the direction of economic activities requires. But in so far as democracy ceases to be a guaranty of individual freedom, it may well persist in some form under a totalitarian regime.

F. A. Hayek (1944)

The revolutionary utopianism of our time invoked a rational methodology and employed pragmatic power in its operations. What resulted was totalitarianism.

Milovan Djilas (1990)

The socialist world is rapidly changing in the 1990s. Marxism is in crisis. The issue over what Marx, a nineteenth-century radical, means today, as we head toward the twenty first century, interests more than academics. It is determining the fate of the Soviet Union and the statist countries of Eastern Europe.

The Soviet Union, in its zest for decentralization, has much to learn from the contemporary history of combining Marxism and self-management. The thirteenth Five Year Plan of the Soviet Union resolves to "Make a radical change in the content and mechanism of centralized planning." But Gorbachev does not want to break completely from the basic Marxist vision. He wishes to return to the "early," more humanistic Marx, the Marx who appealed to workers' self-management. *Perestroika* is pushing in that direction: The Law on General Principles of Local Self-Management and the Local Economy in the USSR calls for the local soviets, the revolutionary workers' councils, to seize power and control day-to-day economic decision-making. Moreover, *perestroika* has created an explosion in the number of cooperative enterprises in the Soviet Union. Cooperatives grew from about 4,000 shortly after the Law on Individual Labor Activity was put into effect on May 1, 1987, to over 51,000, employing more than a million people by the turn of 1990.[1]

Can Gorbachev in the 1990s successfully break from the legacy of Stalinism while remaining faithful to Marxist aspirations, like Yugoslavia's Tito attempted to do in the 1950s? Many of Gorbachev's followers, like the Yugoslav revisionists in the 1950s and 1960s, have rediscovered the young, humanistic Marx of the Paris Manuscripts, the Marx who envisioned an end to worker alienation in all its forms, capitalist and statist. They have rediscovered Karl Marx the radical democrat and decentralist. Can the Gorbachevites find something in Marx that the Yugoslavs missed or misunderstood?

Yugoslavia was supposed to be different, indeed. The League of Communists of Yugoslavia (LCY) launched a long and exhaustive series of economic reforms beginning with the Basic Law on the Management of Economic Enterprises and Higher-Level Economic Associations in 1950, through the introduction of limited market exchange and self-managed investment policies in the 1960s, to the culmination of integrated self-managed socialism with the 1974 Constitution and the 1976 Act of Associated Labor.[2]

The Yugoslav system of socialist self-management is now in an unprecedented state of crisis. It has struggled with the ideal of self-management and the reality of statism for decades. The crucial issue for the Yugoslavs, Gorbachevites, and other Marxists who hold out hope for decentralized, worker-managed socialism is whether the crisis of Yugoslav-style self-management resulted from poor practice and implementation in Yugoslavia itself, or whether it stems from a more fundamental problem of theory and system that goes all the way back to Marx himself.

Modern interpreters of Marx stress an overall unity in his writings, and discredit the orthodox split between the young, humanistic Marx of the 1844 manuscripts and the mature Marx, Marx the economist and materialist, as typified by his *The German Ideology* and *Capital* (cf. Avineri 1968). Although Marx's language changed from the 1840s to the 1860s, the modern interpretation illustrates how Marx's genuine concern for humanism, radical democracy, and the problem of alienation runs throughout his lifelong critique of capitalism. This interpretation is more persuasive than that promoted by earlier orthodox Marxists and Althusserians, who tended to reduce Marx to a materialist and belittle his praxis philosophy as the musings of an immature mind.

But the contemporary crisis of Yugoslav self-management (let alone the totalitarian horror of Stalin's Soviet Union and the former Eastern Bloc) demands that we reconsider Marxism yet again. How can such a consistent, unified thinker become so bastardized in practice? The time has come for a *post*-modern interpretation of Marx, one that helps explain the limits to his radical humanism. Marx strove for a unified humanistic perspective in his writings, and hence he should not be considered an unequivocal advocate of a Stalinesque system of hierarchical "command planning" that coerces and alienates the citizenry. But the self-management alternative and the contradictions exposed in the Yugoslav experience help awaken us to tensions and contradictions that Marx himself had struggled with throughout his career as a thinker and revolutionary.

After briefly discussing the utopian socialists' influence on Marx in chapter 1, I shall demonstrate in chapter 2 that Marx's own utopian, totalistic understanding of the praxis-nature of human beings presumes that he foresaw the possibility of a nonalienated socialist future. He thought that only a comprehensively planned economy with social ownership of the means of production could realize our creative and communal potential. This implies that the system would not be planned and controlled from a commanding center or a bureaucratic hierarchy. Instead, full-fledged socialism would be described as a decentralized, fully participatory, self-managed system.

Yet Marx also developed a sophisticated study of capitalist economic organization. He understood that the overthrow of the market system through comprehensive economic planning would require some sort of central direction. The organizational logic that unfolds when people try to comprehensively plan a technologically developed economy may well point toward complete centralization at the expense of the fully participatory, self-managed ideal.

Although Marx indeed imagined a future socialist utopia where people would concretely fulfill their praxis potential, there rumbles within an essential tension between Marx's praxis philosophy and Marx's organization theory, even though his organization theory is motivated by his praxis critique of alienation. Marx struggled between the humanistic ideal of decentralization and cooperation, and the organizational reality of economic rationalization and centralization.

How should we interpret, for example, Marx's statement from *The Poverty of Philosophy*:

If one took as a model of the division of labor in the modern workshop, in order to apply it to a whole society, the society best organized for the production of wealth would undoubtedly be that which had a single chief employer, distributing tasks to the different members of the community according to some previously fixed rule. (Marx 1978: 125)

Also consider the following statement in *Capital* where he saw the need for organization based upon "one commanding will":

On the one side, all labors, in which many individuals cooperate, necessarily require for the connection and unity of the process one commanding will, and this performs a function, which does not refer to fragmentary operations, but to the combined labor of the workshop, in the same way as does the director of an orchestra. This is a kind of productive labor, which must be performed in every mode of production requiring a combination of labors. (1909, vol. 3: 451; cf. 1906: 363)

Marx elsewhere claimed that "it is very characteristic that the enthusiastic apologists of the factory system have nothing more damning to urge against general organization of the labor of society, than that it would turn all society into one immense factory" (1906: 391). How can these statements be reconciled with Marx's hope for meaningful workers' self-management, for the "republican and beneficent system of the association of free and equal producers" (Marx and Engels 1969, vol. 2: 81)?

Those inclined to emphasize organization theory over praxis philosophy interpret this as Marx's unequivocal call for a central planning board. Paul Craig Roberts (1971), Roberts and Matthew Stephenson (1973), and Don Lavoie (1985c) have written valuable and important works that emphasize the central planning aspects of Marxian socialism, and conclusively demonstrate that Marx called for nothing less than the complete overthrow of the market system. But they have not come to terms with the full praxis implications of central planning.[3] Marx was opposed to both the "anarchy in the social division of labour and despotism in that of the workshop" (1906: 391). To abolish the anarchy of the market system by turning all of society into a despotic, centrally planned factory would (if it worked) subject workers and citizens to a universal capitalist-type boss. Alienation would not end. If the "one commanding will" is merely a substitute slogan for a central planning board, then *de facto* private ownership is retained and the system would be far from socialist. The central planning board would enjoy full disposal over resources. Perhaps this is why Marx finds it necessary to further pursue the orchestra director metaphor: "A director of an orchestra," Marx mentions, "need not be the owner of the instruments of its members, nor is it a part of his function that he should have anything to do with the *wages* of the other musicians" (1909, vol. 3: 455).

Evidently, those who emphasize Marx the organization theorist (as economists tend to do) or Marx the praxis philosopher (as Yugoslav and humanist philosophers tend to do[4]) can find quotes to support their arguments. But an exclusive focus on one side or the other, although once productive for demonstrating the full implications of Marx's organization theory and his praxis philosophy, might now be holding back dialogue in comparative political economy. Economists tend to ignore the full implications of Marx's praxis philosophy and argue that, because the logic of the nonmarket system necessitates central planning, Marx must be considered an advocate of central planning. This argument, however, cannot be reconciled with the foundation of Marx's critique of capitalism—and with it his subsequent call for the outright overthrow of commodity production—because Marx's critique of capitalism is conducted through the spectacles of his praxis philosophy. On the other side, praxis philosophers tend to misunderstand the organizational implications of abolishing the market economy. They therefore seem to believe that the totalitarian centralization of power in "real existing socialism" is little more than bastardized Marxism (though Stojanović's recent work [1988] is a notable exception). In each case, a one-sided interpretation overlooks Marxism's twentieth-century struggle between two opposing forces: the realization of praxis through participation and self-management, and the centralizing demands placed upon the community once the market is largely restricted, if not abolished.

I try to give Marx's research program a hermeneutically open reading in this book. Like other humanists, I share a concern with Marx about many of the coercive institutions and undue authority that our modern age has foisted upon the human lot. But I also believe the Marxist project is utopian and gravely suffers from a knowledge and coordination problem that inevitably appears when socialists attempt to replace the unhampered market process with general economic planning. I shall have occasion to explore in detail the knowledge problem argument developed by the Austrian school of economics in chapter 3.

In chapter 4 I critically assess the contemporary neoclassical economic theory of self-managed socialism. I argue that the propensity among economists to study institutions and complex social processes (such as self-managed enterprises and the pricing system) in a formal, equilibrium model leads them away from some very fundamental questions in comparative political economy. These questions have to do with the nature of economic knowledge and the process by which that knowledge is used and conveyed in the economic system. In chapter 5 I focus on Branko Horvat's case for self-managed socialism and some actual tensions that appear in Yugoslav practice.

Although I argue that workers' self-management is riddled with problems in a socialist or quasi-socialist system, I nevertheless see hope for worker-managed firms in a relatively unhampered market process. In chapter 6 I present a case study of a group of American cooperage (barrel-making) cooperatives that faced extremely tough competitive and technological pressures. They confronted perhaps the worst possible conditions that worker-managed firms are likely to face. And yet the cooperages seem to demonstrate that worker-managed firms are not necessarily backward or inefficient, and, contrary to what some socialists have argued, worker-managed firms can survive and prosper in a market system. I conclude the book by speculating over the future of workers' self-management in our post-Marxist (post–1989) era, and its viability in an unhampered market process.

NOTES

1. The resolution on the thirteenth Five Year Plan is published in *The Current Digest of the Soviet Press*, vol. 42, no. 2 (February 14, 1990), pp. 25-26. That same issue provides the statistics on the number of cooperatives in the Russian Federation as of January 1990 (pp. 33-34). Plokker (1990) provides a good overview of the development of cooperatives since 1987. A discussion of "How Local Soviets Should Seize Power," is published in *The Current Digest of the Soviet Press*, vol. 42, no. 26 (August 1, 1990), pp. 1-4.

2. Yugoslav self-managed socialism was bound for disaster. Yugoslavia's vague notion of "social" ownership, coupled with a lack of unfettered markets for scarce capital goods, would (unsurprisingly) yield utter economic chaos and impending crisis. The extent of the Yugoslav crisis is now well known. Yugoslavia's annual rate of growth in the gross material product averaged 0.7% between 1980–1984, while labor productivity averaged − 1.7% per year during the same period. Yugoslavia's massive foreign debt climbed from 11.8 billion dollars in 1978 to over 21 billion by 1987. The rate of inflation approached 2000% by the end of 1989, while the currency collapsed from 3000 dinars to the U.S. dollar in January 1989 to over 120,000 dinars to the dollar by December 1989. Thousands of strikes have occurred in the past decade, with greater frequency as economic conditions deteriorate. This in turn has fanned the fires of Balkan nationalism (from renewed attempts to rekindle Croat fascism to the growing personality cult of Serbia's Slobodan Milošević and the human rights violations of the ethnic Albanians in Kosovo) and has pushed Yugoslavia to the brink of civil war.

3. In particular, Roberts claims that "in the Marxian scheme, central economic planning eliminates *Marxian* alienation by eliminating the exchange relationships of commodity production" (1971: 10). Lavoie's centralist interpretation of Marxian socialism has been influenced by the Roberts-Stephenson view as well as that of

the earlier Austrian School of economics (cf. Lavoie 1985c: ch. 2). More recently, Andrzey Walicki (1988) also equates Marx with central command planning (see especially p. 34), but Walicki is also aware of Marx's struggle between centralization and decentralization. My earlier piece on Marx (Prychitko 1988) emphasized Marx's praxis-decentralist side, while illustrating the way its tension surfaces in the contemporary blueprint of Michael Albert and Robin Hahnel (1978).

4. The philosophers and other social theorists who have done the most to emphasize the praxis side of Marx are chiefly associated with the Praxis group in Yugoslavia (such as Zagorka Golubović, Danko Grlić, Milan Kangrga, Andrija Krešić, Mihailo Marković, Gajo Petrović, Veljko Rus, Svetozar Stojanović, Rudi Supek, Ljubomir Tadić, and Pedrag Vranicki) and their journal *Praxis* (published between 1965-1974). Fellow travelers included the early Habermas, Erich Fromm, and other East European revisionists such as Agnes Heller and Karel Kosík.

Marxism and Workers' Self-Management

CHAPTER 1 _____

Marx, Utopia, and the Radical Milieu of the Nineteenth Century

The idea of workers managing their own workplaces—cooperation and self-management—has captured the minds of many people. Robert Owen, P. J. B. Buchez, and John Stuart Mill are but a few of the many activists and intellectuals who helped launch the cooperative ideal. History records the Rochdale Pioneers and Owen's New Harmony of the nineteenth century among the first significant episodes in cooperative association. Experiments such as these were influenced by, and in turn had an influence upon, the thinkers, schemers, and dreamers of cooperative association— a give and take between theory and practice.

THE MEANING OF COOPERATIVE PRODUCTION

At its basic level, cooperative production seeks an alternative to the authoritarian structure of the capitalist enterprise by overcoming the division between labor and capital, worker and boss. It seeks to restructure the traditional, hierarchical form of business enterprise by substituting for a despotic boss a constitution that allows workers to democratically participate in the decision-making and control of the enterprise. The cooperative workplace is essentially an alternative form of business organization; it does not necessarily define the characteristics of the overall economic system, because it is but one component.

This has not always been understood. The social implications of cooperative production during the nineteenth century were interpreted differently by various individuals and schools of thought. Interpretations ranged from Charles Barnard's (1881: iv) statement that cooperation "simply means business" (a position which Richard Ely attacked), to Martin Buber's belief that the cooperative experiments of the nineteenth century provided "perfect examples of the inner battle for socialism" (Buber 1958: 70). Motivations ranged from the more practical (protection of jobs, for example) to the more ambitious and ideological (such as the creation of utopian communities). Many experiments in producers' cooperation, such as the cooperage cooperatives of Minneapolis in the late 1800s, were established in the attempt to reduce de-skilling and unstable employment patterns of extremely competitive, technologically advancing markets. Others, such as the Jura watchmakers in Switzerland, or Robert Owen's New Harmony community, were much more ideologically oriented, and often subscribed to, and sometimes further developed, principles of common ownership and applied anarchism.

Many of Marx's predecessors and contemporaries—the anarchists and utopian socialists—spearheaded the European cooperative movement. The ideal of a system of decentralized socialism characterized by workers' self-management has its roots in the intellectual and radical milieu of the nineteenth century, which includes revolutionaries such as P. J. Proudhon, Mikhail Bakunin, and the forerunners of the cooperative movement such as Charles Fourier and Robert Owen. Marx appreciated their call for workers' self-management of industry. But he utterly opposed their methods for attaining socialism. Marx argued that the ideal of self-management and participation could be achieved only after a secure economic foundation is put in place. That foundation requires a centrally organized socialist revolution whereby the proletariat gain control of the state. Anything short of the universal attempt to abolish the anarchy of the market through comprehensive economic planning and a dictatorship of the proletariat would be, in Marx's view, merely utopian.

Marx, of course, became the dominant theoretician and revolutionary on the major scientific issues of socialism, and his influence on contemporary systems of thought in the twentieth century stretches far beyond that of any of the anarchists and utopian socialists. This book critically studies the contemporary models of workers' self-management in a planned, socialist system whose advocates find allegiance in Marx. It is worthwhile, first, to provide a brief sketch of the pre-Marxist and anti-Marxist visions of workers' cooperation and self-management in order to get an idea of the radical milieu that strongly influenced Marx's criticism of capitalism and his vision of socialism.

THE CALL FOR WORKERS' COOPERATION

Charles Fourier (1772-1837) was a major forerunner of the cooperative ideal. In his *La theorie des quatres mouvements*, published in 1808, Fourier envisioned a new system of society, a consciously constructed system of producers' and consumers' cooperatives. A student of Post-Enlightenment, positivist philosophy (he wrote during the development of French Rationalism, generally linked with Henri de Saint-Simon and Auguste Comte), Fourier called for rationally directing the progress of society through comprehensive social reconstruction. Though he did not go as far as Saint-Simon and Comte (who viewed society from the perspective of "social physics"), Fourier nevertheless shared their anxiety over the uncontrolled, spontaneously evolved institutions of industrial capitalism. In his view, the unplanned order of capitalist markets (the "*anarchie industrielle*" of market production, consumption, distribution, and exchange) must be replaced with a planned or "combined" order based upon rational, human design (Fourier 1828). Society would be grouped into controlled, cooperative communities, which Fourier called Phalanxes.

Fourier's Phalanx would replace the anarchic, ungoverned coordination of the market by a deliberate design. This design, based upon the latest developments of expert, scientific reason, would somehow minimize the risk and uncertainty of everyday life. Fourier believed that

a Phalanx *en masse*, directed by its Areopagus of experts, its patriarchs, its neighboring Cantons, and other skilled people, is not liable to imprudence like an individual, and where an industrial undertaking is in any degree adventurous, care is had to distribute the risk involved among a large number of Phalanxes, to deliberate a long time, to obtain insurance, etc.

"As to any risk from knavery," he concluded, "there can be none in Harmony" (Fourier 1971: 188). In this system the labor market would be replaced by a guaranteed right to work, freedom from economic dependence would be the rule, and what was work in capitalist society would become "play" in Fourier's ideal community.

The ideas behind French Rationalism also encouraged P. J. B. Buchez (1796-1865) to promote the development of producers' cooperatives, each a "republic within the workshop," as a catalyst for constructive social change. While Fourier sought to change the system to accord with a fixed human nature, Buchez believed that people will have to change in order for cooperative association to be successful: "Association in work is not possible if each one does not reject egoism, and does not forget himself to think of others." Rather Buchez stressed that, "*Before joining together in association, men need a fundamental change of spirit.*" Moreover, "Such a change is not a matter of one day, nor even a generation" (Buchez quoted in Reibel 1975: 41).

Buchez called upon workers to voluntarily relinquish their personal savings, and raise loans if necessary, to invest in cooperative associations within their particular trade. After each worker receives an equal amount of income, the profits would be left in a common fund, "with the result

that the co-operative workshop becomes a little industrial community."
But Buchez failed to focus upon the overriding structural relationships
between the economy and the state, and thus naively remarked: "let all
the workers do this and the social problem will be solved" (Buchez quoted
in Buber 1958: 66).[1]

In his 1840 classic *L'organisation du travail*, Louis Blanc (1811-1882), a
follower of Buchez, called for nothing less than the elimination of market
competition. Blanc argued that the state must assume responsibility for
sponsoring and financing workers' associations, coordinating economic activities, and distributing income "to each according to his needs, from each
according to his abilities," a phrase which Marx adopted later.

Pierre-Joseph Proudhon (1809-1865) first introduced the term "anarchism" in a non-pejorative sense, which means an orderly society without
a coercive government. His system was mutualist, whereby workers would
emancipate themselves by developing cooperative organizations linked together by equitable exchange relationships (reciprocal "exchange of equivalents") and financed by a centralized, no-interest credit system. The credit
system would be the only explicitly centralized institution in Proudhon's
model. All others are radically decentralized. Though Proudhon had expressed his misgivings over the division of labor and market competition
in the *Systeme des contradictions economiques, ou Philosophie de la misere*
(1846), he did not aim to categorically eliminate them. Rather, Proudhon
wished to preserve the division of labor and rivalrous competition in order
to promote economic coordination and efficiency.

Proudhon's model consisted of spontaneous horizontal relations coupled
with a non-hierarchical political organization. Here "The government is
the public economy, the supreme administration of the labors and goods
of the entire nation." Proudhon the federalist remarked that this nation
"is like a huge corporation in which every citizen is a stockholder" (Proudhon quoted in Commisso 1979: 27). The mutualist associations, based on
the principle of one person, one vote, would try to satisfy the interests of
the workers and justly distribute income. Each association is free to enter
into contracts with others, but these contracts would not be enforced by
a third party (such as the state). Rigorous market competition would provide the appropriate incentives to enter into and maintain contractual
agreements. Indeed, Proudhon believed that spontaneously formed contractual relationships would describe not only the economic sphere traditionally understood, but all spheres of civil and political life.

Proudhon's ideas gained popularity among small peasant proprietors and
skilled craftsmen, such as the watchmakers of the Jura mountains in Switzerland. Mikhail Bakunin (1814-1876), however, was a much more formi-
dable character. He had a particularly direct impact on the Jura Federation,
and became, in opposition to Marx, a leading figure in the First International. The son of an aristocratic Russian landowner, and a member of the

radical Young Hegelians, Bakunin first introduced anarchism as an international revolutionary movement.

In his early work, *Revolutionary Catechism* (1866), Bakunin considered cooperation to be a revolutionary means that could push the world closer to international anarchism: "At this time," Bakunin wrote, "we can only speculate about, but not determine, the immense development that [cooperative workers' associations] will doubtlessly exhibit in the new political and social conditions of the future." He claimed that "they will someday transcend the limits of towns, provinces, and even states." Eventually "They may entirely reconstitute society, dividing it not into nations but into different industrial groups organized not according to the needs of politics but to those of production" (Bakunin 1866: 81-82). But Bakunin espoused collectivism less than a decade later. In *Statism and Anarchy* (1873) he argued that all land and capital must be collectivized before labor could be completely emancipated through cooperative organizations. Bakunin had switched tactics: spontaneous experiments in cooperation would fail to improve the condition of the working masses. Now somewhat influenced by Marx, Bakunin argued that independent producers' cooperatives would not survive among the unabashedly competitive elements of the capitalist system, which concentrate and monopolize capital. Bakunin became convinced that existing cooperatives would merely provide workers with the experience to make democratic production decisions in the workplace. "While cooperation cannot achieve the emancipation of the labouring masses under present socioeconomic conditions," Bakunin argued, "it nevertheless has this advantage, that cooperation can habituate the workers to conduct their own affairs (after the overthrow of the old society)" (Bakunin 1873: 345). In this and other respects, particularly his critique of capitalism, Bakunin was a student of Marx (cf. Saltman 1983: 80-95).

Bakunin strongly disagreed with Marx, however, on the nature of revolution—of the overthrow of the old state—and on the question of revolutionary authority. Marx and Engels argued that the transition from capitalism to socialism required that the bourgeois state be smashed and replaced by a proletarian state. Only afterward, under full-fledged socialism, would the class struggle finally end and the state whither away. Bakunin, here following Proudhon, still advocated the total abolition of the state through a bottom-up revolution, a spontaneous uprising by peasants and poor urban workers. He warned that Marx's call for the dictatorship of the proletariat would fail to liberate the masses, and would instead create a despotism of the revolutionary minority: "If their state would really be of the people, why eliminate it?," Bakunin asked. "And if the State is needed to emancipate the workers, then the workers are not yet free, so why call it a People's State?" Ultimately "every state, not excepting their People's State, is a yoke, on the one hand giving rise to despotism and on the other to slavery" (1873: 331). Bakunin prophetically concluded that "all dictatorship has no other objective than self-perpetuation, and slavery is all it can generate and instill in the people who suffer it. Freedom can be created only by freedom, by a total rebellion of the people, and by voluntary organization of the people from the bottom up" (1873: 332).

Bakunin's anti-authoritarian views unnerved Marx and Engels. In his polemic "On Authority," Frederick Engels attacked Bakunin for denying any and all authority (Marx and Engels 1969, vol. 2: 376-79). But this was a straw man. Bakunin was opposed to the irresponsible, repressive use of authority, not to authority as such. In *God and the State* (published in 1882, six years after he died), Bakunin categorically distinguished authority and authoritarianism. The former arises through persuasive, voluntary action; the latter depends upon the force of coercion (Bakunin 1970: 30-36). Bakunin had rejected authoritarianism. "Does it follow that I reject all authority? Far from me such a thought," he responded. "In the matter of boots, I refer to the authority of the bootmaker; concerning houses, canals, or railroads, I consult that of the architect or engineer. For such or such special knowledge I apply to such or such a *savant*. But I allow neither the bootmaker nor the architect nor the *savant* to impose his authority on me." Engels erroneously dismissed this as mere semantics. Bakunin's argument that under mutual exchange "there is no fixed and constant authority, but a continual exchange of mutual, temporary, and above all, voluntary authority and subordination," is, however, consistent with a contemporary, post-positivist philosophy of knowledge as expressed in the work of Hans-Georg Gadamer and should be considered much more seriously than Marx, Engels, and their disciples have been willing to do.[2] At any rate, whether one agrees with Bakunin or not, his insistence on an anti-authoritarian anarchist revolution clearly distinguishes him from Marx and Engels on the issue of the transition to comprehensive self-management.

The earliest and most influential advocate of cooperative association outside the Continent was, without doubt, Robert Owen (1771-1858). Owen differed from the French Rationalists in the following way: Saint-Simon and Fourier sought to construct a new society in order to bring individuals into harmony with what they argued was an innate human nature. Owen argued in *A New View of Society, or Essays on the Formation of Human Character* (1817) that human nature is a product of our environment, and he therefore sought to reform institutions in order to reform people.[3] Owen practiced his simple philosophy by managing the New Lanark textile mills in Scotland, which improved workers' housing conditions, reduced the length of the workday, improved children's education and abolished child labor. That helped popularize his ideas. He did not, however, convince the British aristocracy of the value of his proposed reforms for a society-wide level, and thus embarked to the United States in 1824 to establish a cooperative community in New Harmony, Indiana.

Owen considered New Harmony a "New Moral World," one which was organized "to rationally educate and employ all, through a new organization of society which will give a new existence to man by surrounding him with superior circumstances only" (Owen quoted in Lockwood 1905: 59; cf. Carpenter 1972: 1-35). Although the experiment was, in fact, not very successful, it encouraged the formation of several other experimental communities.

Owen later returned to Britain, after which his ideas sparked the formation of the successful Rochdale Pioneers' Cooperative Society in 1844, an organization that still flourishes today as a consumers' cooperative. But, for the most part, Owen's vision of social reform simply stimulated working class radicals who were more interested in forming producer cooperatives as alternatives to boss shops, and less interested in creating utopian communities.

MARX, PRODUCERS' COOPERATIVES, AND SCIENTIFIC SOCIALISM

Surely the humanistic ideals of the anarchists and utopian socialists influenced Marx. One need only consider Engels' glowing discussion in *Anti-Dühring* (1978: 309-22), written at Marx's request. Occasionally Marx even acknowledged some value of cooperative labor under capitalism. When he established the First Congress of the International Working Men's Association in 1866, for instance, Marx encouraged workers to embark upon cooperative production. Though he intentionally avoided any details about a particular system of cooperation, Marx said (in his "Instructions for the Delegates of the Provisional General Council: The Different Questions") that

We acknowledge the co-operative movement as one of the transforming forces of the present society based upon class antagonism. Its great merit is to practically show, that the present pauperising, and despotic system of the *subordination of labour* to capital can be superseded by the republican and beneficent system of the association of free and equal producers.

He was quick to point out, however, the possible dangers that producers' cooperatives might degenerate into joint stock companies; but he merely concluded that all workers "ought to share alike" in order to reduce this risk (Marx and Engels 1969, vol. 2: 77-85).

Marx nevertheless maintained that cooperative production would not, in itself, "convert social production into one large and harmonious system of free and co-operative labour." Rather, he stressed that *"general social changes are wanted, changes of the general conditions of society*, never to be realized save by the transfer of the organised forces of society, viz., the

state power, from the capitalists and landlords to the producers themselves"
(1969, vol. 2: 81-82). Only a utopian would believe otherwise. Referring
specifically to Owen (but intended to apply to all those who fell short of
the call for comprehensive planning), Marx wrote in *Capital* that "directly
associated labor [is] a form of production that is entirely inconsistent with
the production of commodities" (1906, vol. 1: 106, n. 1). The general social
changes will arrive. Marx maintained, only after the workers themselves
usurp the power of the state.[4]

Marx was particularly impressed with the Paris Commune of 1871, as
expressed in *The Civil War in France* (Marx and Engels 1969, vol. 2: 202-
44). Although it lasted only two months, the Commune had abolished
conscription and the standing army, and attempted to establish producers'
cooperatives within industry. Industries would in turn be organized into a
federation of cooperatives. Universal suffrage would rule, with decision-
making resting among the workers or their elected representatives, who
were subject to recall. Public service was to be done at workmen's wages
(cf. Edwards 1973).

The majority of the Commune's members were followers of Louis-Au-
guste Blanqui (1805–1881), the socialist revolutionary admired by Marx
and Engels; the minority were followers of Proudhon. Marx and Engels
delighted in the fact that the Commune, they (perhaps strategically)
claimed, seemed more a product of Marxist thinking than that of the
Blanquists and Proudhonists. They created a system much to Marx's satisfaction:

The Commune, they exclaim, intends to abolish property, the basis of all civ-
ilisation! Yes, gentlemen, the Commune intended to abolish that class-property
which makes the labour of the many the wealth of the few. It aimed at the expro-
priation of the expropriators. It wanted to make individual property a truth by
transforming the means of production, land and capital, now chiefly the means of
enslaving and exploiting labour, into mere instruments of free and associated labour.—But this is Communism, "impossible" Communism! Why, those members
of the ruling classes who are intelligent enough to perceive the impossibility of
continuing the present system—and they are many—have become the obtrusive
and full-mouthed apostles of co-operative production. If co-operative production
is not to remain a sham and a snare; if it is to supersede the Capitalist system; if
united co-operative societies are to regulate national production upon a common
plan, thus taking it under their own control, and putting an end to the constant
anarchy and periodical convulsions which are the fatality of Capitalist production—
what else, gentlemen, would it be but Communism, "possible" Communism? (1969,
vol. 2: 223-24)

Thus Marx had acknowledged the Paris Commune, with its federation of
cooperative organs, as authentic communism, a "glorious harbinger of a
new society" (p. 241).

Marx chided the utopians because they failed to provide a systematic account of the evils they observed under capitalism. They simply proposed intricately detailed blueprints of the ideal socialist society, blueprints which would be rationally constructed on the basis of scientific reason.[5] Although they recognized class antagonism in society, they were "utopians" because they failed to see history itself as a class struggle. They did not understand how the class struggle determined the conditions for social change. Hence, the utopians could not understand the revolutionary role of the proletariat in accomplishing the transition from capitalism to socialism. "Historical action," wrote Marx and Engels, "is to yield to their personal inventive action, historically created conditions of emancipation to fantastic ones, and the gradual, spontaneous class-organization of the proletariat to an organization of society specially contrived by these inventors." For the utopian socialists, "Future history resolves itself . . . into the propaganda and the practical carrying out of their plans" (1969, vol. 1: 134).

The utopian socialists may have been fantastic dreamers, but they were far from irrelevant. The utopians mattered a great deal to Marx and Engels. They considered the utopians utter pests who obstructed fundamental social change. They write that the utopians

endeavor, and that consistently, to deaden the class struggle and to reconcile the class antagonisms. They still dream of experimental realisation of their social Uto-pias, of founding isolated *"phalansteres,"* of establishing "Home Colonies," of setting up a "Little Icaria"—duodecimo editions of the New Jerusalem. . . . By degrees they sink into the category of the reactionary conservative Socialists . . . differing from these only by more systematic pedantry, and by their fanatical and superstitious belief in the miraculous effects of their social science. (1969, vol. 1: 135-36)

Marx and Engels proposed, instead, "scientific" socialism. As they described it, scientific socialism does not attempt to discuss all the details of the future socialist society, but instead offers a general vision of fully developed socialism through a radical and comprehensive critique of existing capitalism (1969, vol. 1: 98-137; 1970: 115-51).

Scientific socialism appealed to the positivistic notion of science rapidly developing during the mid to late nineteenth century, and Marx was able to appropriate the ideology of positivism and scientism to dismiss his fellow socialist adversaries as nonscientific, nonsensical utopians. Who would listen to a utopian in an age of modern science? His strategy worked: Marx won favor of many "scientifically minded" socialists and revolutionaries who wished to gain control of the state.

But Marx himself harbored a utopian understanding of human essence implied in his notion of praxis. Praxis is the benchmark that he uses to radically criticize capitalism, and to inform us of the general features of complete socialism. Although Marx's life-work seems to be a unified project based upon his understanding of people as beings of praxis, it is nevertheless wrought with a fundamentally inherent struggle—an essential tension—between his vision of the ideal socialist future and the organizational realities of comprehensive economic planning.

NOTES

1. R. Reibel points out that Buchez's notion of the workingman's association "demanded an extremely developed spirit of charity, especially on the part of its founders," because the fruits of their investment would be enjoyed primarily by future generations alone. Reibel argues that this feature is nevertheless "indispensable" because it "gives the 'revolutionary' value to the association by making it an instrument of liberation of wage-earners" (1975: 42). But self-management in contemporary Yugoslavia has been troubled by this intergenerational problem as well, which has prompted state-mandated investment. That, in turn, has helped destroy the autonomy and "revolutionary value" of the self-managed enterprise.

2. Gadamer maintains that authority "rests on recognition and hence on an act of reason itself which, aware of its own limitations, accepts that others have better understanding. Authority in this sense, properly understood, has nothing to do with blind obedience to a command. Indeed, authority has nothing to do with obedience, but rather with knowledge" (Gadamer 1985: 248). "True authority," Gadamer concludes, "does not have to be authoritarian" (1985: 524, n. 187). Unfortunately, many contemporary collectivist organizations still fail to make this distinction, and wish to abolish all authority relations. For an example, see Rothschild and Whitt (1986: 50-52).

3. Owen remarks:

every day will make it more and more evident that the character of man is, without a single exception, always formed for him; that it may be, and is chiefly, created by his predecessor; that they give him, or may give him, his ideas and habits, which are the powers that govern and direct his conduct. Man, therefore, never did, nor is it possible he ever can, form his own character. (1817: 91-92)

Marx explicitly criticized Owen here. In his third thesis on Feuerbach, Marx claims "it is men that change circumstances" through revolutionary praxis (Marx and Engels 1969, vol. 1: 13). I shall discuss Marx's notion of human nature as praxis in the next chapter.

4. When Marx wrote the *Critique of the Gotha Program* (1875) to distinguish his position from the Lasalleans, he once again demonstrated the futility of attempting to totally transform society by establishing producers' cooperative societies, even if financed by the state. Marx valued existing cooperative associations only to the extent that they were independently established by workers, free from the state or the bourgeoisie. As he said of Lasalle: "This is worthy of [Lasalle's] imagination that one can build a new society by state loans just as well as a new railway." Instead, Marx insisted that the transformation of society can come about only through revolution. (See Marx and Engels 1970: 13-30.)

5. Intricate they were indeed. Fourier, for example, envisioned a socialist utopia

containing exactly 2,985,984 phalanxes, each composed of 1,600 people who would be responsible for cultivating 5,000 acres of land, whereby five-twelfths of income would be distributed to manual labor, four-twelfths to invested capital, and three-twelfths to theoretical and practical knowledge. His blueprint of Harmony goes into ever more minute details, such as his discussion concerning the gastronomic categories that the different members of the phalanx would fall into, and the details of food preparation and kitchen table management (Beecher and Bienvenu 1983: 251-52, 265-70). If that was not enough to rattle Marx, Fourier verged on outright lunacy. He claimed that when society reaches Harmony, the sea will turn into lemonade, six new moons will appear, everyone will live to be 144 years old, and new animals will appear, such as anti-lions, anti-whales, anti-bears, anti-bugs, and anti-rats (see Heilbroner 1967: 112). Little wonder Marx would condemn the methods of the utopians.

CHAPTER 2 _____

The Essential Tension: Praxis, Cooperation, and Comprehensive Planning in Marxian Socialism

MARX'S NOTION OF PRAXIS

Marx attacked classical political economy as vehemently as he attacked the utopian socialists. He claimed that the classical economists never tried to comprehend capitalist institutions such as private property, money, competition, and capital. Instead, classical economists simply treated these institutions as given. "Political economy starts with the fact of private property," wrote Marx in *Economic and Philosophic Manuscripts of 1844,*

but it does not explain it to us. It expresses in general, abstract formulas the *material* process through which private property actually passes, and these formulas it then takes for *laws*. It does not *comprehend* these laws, i.e., it does not demonstrate how they arise from the very nature of private property. (1964: 106)

In addition, "political economy does not disclose the source of the division between labor and capital, and between capital and land. . . . it takes for granted what it is supposed to explain. Similarly, competition comes in everywhere. It is explained from external circumstances."[1] Marx's main concern is to comprehend the laws of capitalism and to offer an account of the nature of its institutions.

Marx develops a philosophy of *human being*. He argues that a person is a being of praxis, or action. Since Aristotle, praxis generally referred to practice, or human action. But Marx interprets the concept to mean that people are constituted as free, creative beings. Our purposive activity allows us to design the future and the world we live in. It is the fundamental element of our "species-being," and distinguishes human from animal, for only a human is a being of praxis. Hence Marx writes in *Capital*:

We presuppose labour in a form that stamps it as exclusively human. A spider conducts operations that resemble those of a weaver, and a bee puts to shame many an architect in the construction of her cells. But what distinguishes the worst architect from the best of bees is this, that the architect raises his structure in his imagination before he erects it in reality. At the end of every labour-process, we get a result that already existed in the imagination of the labourer at its commencement. (Marx 1906: 198)

This does not mean, however, that we realize our full praxis potential, our essence, in capitalist society. For Marx, we lack authentic praxis in a market system, the overall integration of which is not purposefully designed in advance, but better described, as Marx so often did, as being "anarchic," or ungoverned.

For Marx, praxis is an ontological notion, a claim about human essence.[2] But it has a pragmatic use as well. Marx uses the praxis concept as a foil and a benchmark to analyze and critically evaluate the human condition in modern capitalist society. The praxis foil allows Marx to criticize capitalism in terms of estrangement, or alienation.[3]

People are estranged or alienated when they are blocked from realizing their praxis potential. In the Paris Manuscripts, Marx points to several forms of economic estrangement. The first is the estrangement of workers from the product of their labor. Workers confront the product not as their own free creation, but a thing outside of them, out of their control, as "something hostile and alien" (1964: 108). Ultimately, capitalists, not workers, enjoy the fruits of the workers' labor power. This implies, secondly, that the act of production itself must also alienate people. The act of production does not promise to be a fountainhead of creative activity for the worker. It is instead "an activity which is turned against him, independent of him and not belonging to him," because the worker is subject to the despotic control of the capitalist manager (pp. 111-12).

Workers are not yet free, creative producers under capitalism. They are forced to sell their labor power to capitalists for a money wage (a subsistence wage in long run equilibrium). Labor power itself is a commodity, an object of purchase and sale in the labor market. Workers do not produce to satisfy the creative aspect of their being. They labor merely to survive. Marx therefore insists that the worker's productive activity is "not voluntary, but coerced; it is *forced labor*."[4] Moreover, workers receive the means to sustain life not from nature, but from capitalists in the form of a money wage. No longer providing the means of life for workers, nature itself confronts people as something alien.

A person, then, is estranged from the object of his or her labor, the production process, and from nature. But because a person is a species-being, a being of praxis, a potentially free, creative being, then a person is also estranged "from himself" under capitalism. He is not yet free to enjoy the historical potential that awaits him. He does not realize his praxis. Estranged from oneself, it follows that a person is alienated from other people, confronting them instrumentally, as mere objects, not as autonomous, creative beings.[5]

Of course, not only is the laborer estranged. So, too, is the capitalist. Estranged labor is an alienated *activity*; estrangement for the non-laborer is an alienated *state of affairs* (p. 119). This is perhaps expressed best in the social division of labor.[6]

MARX ON DIVISIONS OF LABOR

Marx distinguishes between the division of labor in the firm and in society as a whole.[7] They differ in the following way. The division of labor within the firm is a detailed project of the capitalist's imagination. It is a structure that is rationally designed before production takes place to assure the most efficient combination of labor and other scarce resources. It is enforced through the despotic control of the capitalist.

The division of labor within the firm reflects the capitalist's general production plan. The social division of labor, on the other hand, is a product of anarchy. It unfolds in a spontaneous, undesigned fashion, an outcome of rivalrous buying and selling within the market process.[8] Its complexity attests to the inevitable clashing of millions of independent plans that results when capital is widely distributed.

Marx, therefore, argues that the two divisions of labor differ in degree and kind. The division of labor within the capitalist firm is rationally determined in advance and "externally" imposed upon workers by the authority of the capitalist, while that within society results from a battle among millions of individual plans, imposed "externally" upon all by the market process. Marx rightly sees the "anarchy in the social division of labor and despotism in that of the workshop" as two very different phenomena from the standpoint of economic organization (1906: 391).

Both are equally destructive from the point of view of human praxis. Though the worker faces an alienating force within the enterprise, worker and capitalist alike confront the alien, uncontrollable force of the social division of labor. Referring to the social division of labor in *The German Ideology*, Marx argues that "division of labour and private property are, moreover, identical expressions: in the one the same thing is affirmed with reference to activity as is affirmed in the other with reference to the product of activity" (Marx and Engels 1969, vol. 1: 34). Hence, the division of labor implies the contradiction between the interest of the separate individual or the individual family and the common interest of all individuals who have intercourse with one another. And indeed, this communal interest does not exist merely in the imagination, as the 'general interest,' but first of all in reality, as the mutual interdependence of the individuals among whom the labour is divided. (p. 34)

The social division of labor integrates economic relationships. It is something of a socioeconomic mosaic. It puts people in their place. Viewed from the praxis foil, however, it is a crude, violent procedure for economic coordination, one that coercively severs individual and common interests. In a popular passage in *The German Ideology* Marx compares the involuntary and uncontrollable nature of the spontaneously formed social division of labor to that which would be voluntarily planned:

And finally, the division of labour offers us the first example of how, as long as man remains in natural society, that is, as long as a cleavage exists between the particular and the common interest, as long, therefore, as activity is not voluntarily, but naturally, divided, man's own deed becomes an alien power opposed to him, which enslaves him instead of being controlled by him. For as soon as the distribution of labour comes into being, each man has a particular, exclusive sphere of activity, which is forced upon him and from which he cannot escape. He is a hunter, a fisherman, a shepherd, or a critical critic, and must remain so if he does not want to lose his means of livelihood; while in communist society, where nobody has one exclusive sphere of activity but each can become accomplished in any branch he wishes, society regulates the general production and thus makes it possible for me to do one thing today and another tomorrow, to hunt in the morning, fish in the afternoon, rear cattle in the evening, criticize after dinner, just as I have in mind, without ever becoming hunter, fisherman, shepherd, or critic. (pp. 35-36)

This passage, which hints of Fourier, underscores one of Marx's central concerns: the hope for a voluntarily controlled social division of labor, and the freedom from a hierarchically determined division of labor in the enterprise.

COMMODITY PRODUCTION

Marx argues that the evolution of the commodity form changed the nature of the social division of labor from a simple, purposefully controlled institution to a coercive, spontaneous order. It is also responsible for the despotically controlled division of labor in the enterprise (Marx 1906: 394).

Marx's discussion of commodity production in *Capital* is still informed by his image of people as praxis beings. Marx focuses on commodity production in his later work because he recognizes commodity production is universal under capitalism. But he does not abandon the praxis foil. Rather, he draws our attention to what he believes is the most comprehensive expression of estranged labor to date—universal, thoroughly anarchic commodity production. Equally important, it is capitalism's key organizing principle.

In any economic system, the product of labor is a use value. But with the ever-expanding institution of exchange, which reaches its zenith under conditions of comprehensive monetary exchange, the product of labor becomes entirely expressed as a commodity with exchange value. In other words, production for exchange, for monetary profit, replaces production for use.

Exchange value, says Marx, converts the products of labor into a "social hieroglyphic." Monetary exchange "conceals, instead of disclosing, the social character of private labor, and the social relations between the individual producers" (1906: 87). Although the division of labor within the enterprise becomes ever more rationalized (the result of an increasingly detailed, scientific plan), the relationships between enterprises become all the more haphazard and wasteful: "the behaviour of men in the social process of production," Marx observes, "is purely atomic." The economic relationships between enterprises "assume a material character independent of their control and conscious individual action" (1906: 105). Marx believes he has exposed a contradiction: "While inside the modern workshop the division of labour is meticulously regulated by the authority of the employer, modern society has no other rule, no other authority for the distribution of labor than free competition" (1978: 125). Marx attempts to explain the anarchic organization of capitalism by pointing to its fundamental element—the production and circulation of commodities.

Individuals enter the market process not as men and women, but as owners of commodities. What was once a mutual interdependence of individuals is, in capitalism, a mutual dependence of individuals through their exchange of commodities (1906: 121). Marx presents this argument with the schema C—M—C, where C denotes the commodity form and M the money form. Exchange is a process of converting C into M and then M into C. In a market situation, individuals confront one another as buyer and seller. Someone has a commodity she wishes to sell; another, holding money, wishes to purchase the commodity. They strike up a price and a sale is made.

From the commodity owner's perspective, she sells the commodity for a cash equivalent, which on average and in equilibrium represents its value in exchange. Say, for example, she sells a pair of shoes for forty dollars. She exchanges the commodity form for the money form, which Marx represents as one side of the relationship C—M. C (one pair of shoes) transforms into M (forty dollars). From the buyer's perspective, he releases money and receives in return the commodity he desires. He converts money into a commodity, transforming M (forty dollars) into C (one pair of shoes).[9] But we have not completed the formula C—M—C, for we are considering a process whereby an individual transforms a specific commodity into money, then uses that money to purchase a different commodity. Though the transaction begins with the sale of the commodity, C—M, it does not end there. Rather, the sale leads to the purchase of another commodity.

The metamorphosis is complete only after the individual who sold the pair of shoes for forty dollars now purchases, say, an umbrella for the same price. The metamorphosis is thus represented as C (shoes)—M (forty dollars)—C (umbrella). Now the circuit is complete.

But the process has not ended. Because every purchase is a sale, and vice versa, the purchase M—C implies yet another sale C—M, which is to say, continuing the example, the seller of the umbrella now attempts to purchase a different commodity (a restaurant dinner, for example). "Hence the circuit made by one commodity," Marx explains, "is inextricably mixed up with the circuits of other commodities" (1906: 126).

The uncontrollable outcomes of commodity exchange are apparent. Each purchase and sale sets into motion a chain of events, events which, in their totality, cannot be fully anticipated by the individual market participants. And to compound this, Marx considers yet another characteristic of the system: the circulation of capital. Here, money capital is transformed into commodities, with the purpose of transforming the commodities back into money, a procedure which Marx denotes as M—C—M.[10] Under commodity production the metamorphosis requires a three-stage process. The capitalist must purchase the labor power of the worker, M—C, which is used to produce a new commodity, C'. That new commodity, the property of the capitalist, is then sold in the market, providing M' in return to the capitalist. This Marx represents by M—C . . . P . . . C'—M' (1909, vol. 2: ch. 1). The capitalist retains his authoritarian, despotic control in the production process, P, which transforms C into C'. But the circulation of commodities (the purchase of labor power, M—C, and the sale of the final product, C'—M') always confronts the capitalist as an alien will, "as an independent substance, endowed with a motion all its own, passing through a life-process of its own, in which money and commodities are mere forms which it assumes and casts off in turn" (1906: 172).

Marx therefore points to the commodity mode of production as the fundamental organizing principle in capitalist society. Commodity production is not necessarily always chaotic. After all, capitalism is not in a state of continuous economic crisis. Rather, Marx's focus on commodity production helps him explain the fundamental nature of capitalist crisis. Specifically, crisis results from the irrational, unplanned and uncontrollable workings of commodity production.[11] Ultimately, for Marx, only the complete elimination of commodity production through participatory comprehensive planning will put an end to alienation and economic crises.

SCIENTIFIC SOCIALISM AS SYSTEMS ANALYSIS

Marx viewed capitalism as the most comprehensively developed system of commodity production. The power of the capitalist in the workshop, and the sweeping, uncontrollable laws of capitalist markets, led Marx to conclude that men and women are anything but free, creative beings. From the praxis benchmark, the commodity mode of production, capitalism's fundamental organizational form, is the most powerful force blocking the fulfillment of human freedom.

On the surface, it may seem that Marx has little to say about the economics of socialism. No doubt socialism would reintegrate or "return man to himself" (1964: 135). But, in the name of scientific socialism, Marx offers no detailed blueprint of the future socialist community. Given the radical transformation that must take place, it is no more than fantasy, a guessing game for utopians, to adequately describe the details of the socialist future.

Marx proposes instead a scientific socialism, which, by self-description, offers a radical criticism of existing capitalism rather than a detailed proposal for socialism. It would be mistaken to conclude, however, that Marx is silent on socialist economic organization.[12] He does not discuss market alienation for the sake of description alone. His use of praxis and his critique of alienation are necessarily revolutionary, and imply a *general* idea of the socialist future. As Gajo Petrović states:

Marx's conception of man can never remain only a conception. Only to conceive man would mean only to conceive what man already was. But man is not only what he has been; he is in the first place what he can and ought to be. Marx's turn to praxis follows from this in the sense that his conception of man cannot remain a mere conception, but it is also a criticism of alienated man who does not realize his human possibilities and a humanistic program of struggle for humanness. Marx's conception of man can thus not be separated from his humanistic theory of alienation and de-alienation. (1967: 80-81)

This is not an isolated interpretation.[13] One could tease out the implications that Marx's critique of market alienation has for socialist economic organization. As Don Lavoie points out, "Marx's scientific socialism was not merely an excuse for avoiding any examination of socialist society. It was a recommendation of a particular method for the conduct of such an examination—that is, that socialism be described through a systematic critique of capitalism" (1985c: 29).

Marx's critique of capitalism is informed by his vision of the socialist future. The socialist future must be that which emancipates people from the alienating aspects of capitalist economic organization. In particular, the socialist future must be that which overcomes the gap between human essence and existence, and thus fulfills our praxis—our potential to be truly free and creative. Socialism allows what would otherwise be an arbitrary construct, the praxis notion, to become something real and concrete (cf. Golubović 1985).[14]

THE PRAXIS OF PARTICIPATORY PLANNING

Because Marx considers socialism to be the system that allows people to "return" to themselves (to fulfill their praxis-nature), then capitalism's alienating, anarchic, involuntary institutions must be abolished outright and replaced by a comprehensive, rational plan. In other words, Marx's view of socialism does indeed carry a strong message about the organization of economic activity.

Marx believes this to be an ever greater possibility as capitalism progresses, because that which generates an ever increasing social division of labor—widely distributed capital—becomes increasingly concentrated in the form of monopoly capitalism; and that which supports the division of labor in the firm—a concentration of capital—is eroded by joint stock companies, banking, and credit. These economic conditions, argues Marx, allow for the revolutionary overthrow of capitalism, and ultimately, comprehensive planning.

In fact, Marx occasionally hints at comprehensive planning throughout his work. In the first volume of *Capital*, for instance, Marx imagines "a community of free individuals, carrying on their work with the means of production in common," not spontaneously, but "in accordance with a definite social plan" (1906: 90). Marx believes that "the life-process of society, which is based on the process of material production, does not strip off its mystical veil until it is treated as production by freely associated men, and is consciously regulated by them in accordance with a settled plan" (p. 92). Only then will market alienation end, which allows people to become free. For Marx:

The freedom in this field cannot consist of anything else but of the fact that socialized man, the associated producers, regulate their interchange with nature rationally, bring it under their common control, instead of being ruled by it as by some blind power; that they accomplish their task with the least expenditure of energy and under conditions most adequate to their human nature and most worthy of it. But it always remains a realm of necessity. Beyond it begins that development of human power, which is its own end, the true realm of freedom, which, however, can flourish only upon the realm of necessity as its basis. The shortening of the working day is its fundamental premise. (1909, vol. 3: 954)

Consequently, Marx believes socialism will negate the uncontrollable institution of commodity production and exchange. It follows that production for the market will be fully replaced by production for direct use;

exchange value will give way to use value; money will cease to function; the division between capital and labor will cease as production takes place through workers' cooperatives; the means of production will be brought under common economic control; and, just as the architect imagines a detailed plan before he commences construction, so, too, will the associated producers participate in creating the social mosaic of their choosing, by creating a unified plan.

Planning will be accomplished, Marx explains, "under conditions most adequate to their human nature and most worthy of it." Human nature, for Marx, is praxis-nature.[15] Hence, what was only an historical, albeit crucial, potential for free, creative activity under capitalism now becomes concrete under socialism.

Only by using praxis as a philosophical concept can Marx interpret capitalism in terms of estrangement and alienation (or abstract labor, commodity fetishism, etc.). These categories lose their critical force, indeed they become arbitrary, if Marx does not constantly rely upon the notion of a non-estranged, freely creative person. Moreover, Marx's own use of praxis is revolutionary in that it implies that people can, and will, fulfill their nature as beings of praxis: under socialism we "return to ourselves," as it were.

Socialism as the fulfillment of praxis suggests that the "contradiction" between wage labor and capital will be abolished, and therefore points toward workers' self-management, whereby the production process within the workplace will come under the common control of the workers themselves. The largely unsubtle form of political exploitation between boss and worker would cease to exist. Also, because the commodity mode of production, whose prime mover is exchange value and monetary calculation, represents the most developed expression of estrangement, it only makes sense that this anarchic, spontaneously created market institution would cease to exist under socialism. Hence, socialism would be further characterized as an economic system that replaces the subtle economic exploitation of unplanned, uncontrollable markets with a comprehensive, rational plan.

Marx's use of the praxis benchmark to critically study capitalism implies that he must have expected the socialist future would be fully compatible with the concrete realization of praxis-nature, and must eventually eliminate political and economic alienation.

Paul Craig Roberts has argued, however, that Marx's wish to abolish the commodity mode of production points to socialism as a centrally planned command system. He writes:

Marx's interpretation of alienation is unique in that he sees the phenomenon as being a product of the developed market system. The method of economic organization enslaves both workers and capitalists. The unique character of Marxian alienation permits a unique solution. Organization of autonomous producers in a system of market relationships is replaced by uniting the whole of society into a single factory.

We are not positing the truth about alienation or claiming that central planning actually would eliminate alienation. We are merely saying that in the Marxian scheme, central planning eliminates *Marxian* alienation by eliminating the exchange relationships of commodity production, that is, we are merely offering an interpretation of Marx. (1971: 10)[16]

I agree with the Roberts-Stephenson-Lavoie argument that socialism must abolish the commodity mode of production, money, exchange, and so on. I nevertheless believe their interpretation of Marx as a necessary advocate of hierarchical central planning is incorrect. Marx was an advocate of participatory but (somehow) unified planning. It may turn out that the only way to achieve the unity of planning Marx wants is to resort to centralization and hierarchy, but Marx did not advocate this.[17]

Their interpretation of Marx's meaning of alienation seems too economistic.[18] Though they have done a great service by presenting Marx as an organization theorist, their exclusive focus on economic organization leads them to neglect the other side of Marx: Marx the praxis philosopher.

Roberts and Stephenson rightly recognize that "in Marx's scheme, alienation is not overcome until capitalism is destroyed and planned production for direct use takes the place of production for the market." But, because they are concerned only with subtle, economic alienation, they neglect what lies behind that—Marx's philosophical understanding of praxis and its implications for economic *and* political alienation. Roberts and Stephenson simply conclude: "When exchange ceases, so does alienation" (p. 93). Although that may be a necessary condition for de-alienation, it is certainly not sufficient. The "alien will" of market exchange activity must not be abolished and substituted by another alien will, such as an inhuman, all-powerful central planning bureaucracy.

Marx's study of alienation goes well beyond that of economic estrangement. His *Critique of Hegel's 'Philosophy of Right'*, for example, powerfully attacks political alienation. By way of criticizing Hegel's political philosophy and defense of the Prussian monarchy, Marx focuses on the alienating opposition between the modern state and civil society. "The state becomes something alien to the nature of civil society; it becomes this nature's otherworldly realm of deputies which makes claims against society" says Marx (1970: 50). Thus, "the separation of civil society and the political state appears necessarily to be a separation of the political citizen, the citizen of the state, from civil society, i.e., from his own actual, empirical reality; for as a state-idealist he is a being who is completely other, distinct, different from and opposed to his own actuality" (p. 78).[19]

Roberts and Stephenson write that because "many think that Marx's concept of communism is nonhierarchical," they "have failed to understand Marx's idea of freedom under communism" (1973: 29-30). But perhaps the authors themselves overlook Marx's damning critique of hierarchy and bureaucracy, a critique which is worth quoting at length:

The aims of the state are transformed into aims of bureaus, or the aims of bureaus into aims of the state. The bureaucracy is a circle from which no one can escape. Its hierarchy is a hierarchy of knowledge. The highest point entrusts the understanding of particulars to the lower echelons, whereas these, on the other hand, credit the highest with an understanding in regard to the universal; and thus they deceive one another. (1970: 47)

Criticizing Hegel, Marx writes that, according to Hegel,

the security of the state and its subjects against the misuse [den Missbrauch] of power by ministers and their officials lies partly in their hierarchical organization (as if the hierarchy itself were not the principle abuse [der Hauptmissbrauch], and the matching personal sins of the civil servants were not at all to be compared with their inevitable hierarchical sins; the hierarchy punishes the civil servant to the extent that he sins against the hierarchy or commits a sin in excess of the hierarchy; but it takes him under its protection when the hierarchy sins through him; moreover the hierarchy is only with great difficulty convinced of the sins of its members) and in the authority given to societies and Corporations, because in itself this is a barrier against the intrusion of subjective caprice into the power entrusted to a civil servant, and it completes from below the state control (as if this control were not exercised without the outlook of the bureaucratic hierarchy) which does not reach down as far as the conduct of individuals. (pp. 52-53)

Marx concludes:

Thus, if we ask Hegel what is civil society's protection against bureaucracy, he answers:
(1) The hierarchical organization of the bureaucracy. *Control.* This, that the adversary is himself bound hand and foot, and if he is like a hammer *vis-a-vis* those below he is like an anvil in relation to those above. Now, where is the protection against the hierarchy? The lesser evil will surely be abolished through the greater inasmuch as it vanishes in comparison with it.
(2) *Conflict*, the unresolved conflict between bureaucracy and Corporation. *Struggle*, the possibility of struggle, is the guarantee against being overcome. Later (para. 297) in addition to this Hegel adds as guarantee the 'institutions [of] the sovereign working . . . at the top,' by which is to be understood, once again, the hierarchy. (p. 53)

Marx is thus well aware of the contradictions inherent in modern bureaucracy, and the alien power it has over people. He explicitly considers the extent to which individuals should participate in political matters of general concern, and calls for universal suffrage in order to abolish the estrangement which is the product of the opposing dualism between the private and public spheres of life.

The state, which, like religion, assumes an alien power, forces the citizen into an atomistic, limited mode of being, and thereby deprives him or her of the social activity to participate in issues of universal importance. "Man's content," says Marx, "is not taken to be his true actuality" (p. 82). Because "the question whether all as individuals should share in deliberating and deciding on matters of general concern is a question that arises from the separation of the political and civil society" (p. 118), Marx calls for nothing less than radical democracy: "in true democracy the *political state disappears*" (p. 31). This abolishes the bifurcation of peoples' social lives, brings together the public and private spheres, and allows people to achieve their species-will, or their drive for full participation in communal affairs (pp. 118-19).

Marx insists hierarchy is a deceiving hierarchy of knowledge. He exposes the schism whereby those at the top are supposed to know universals while those at the bottom are supposed to know particulars. A hierarchy of knowledge represents, for Marx, yet another cleavage between the particular and common interest. Merely democratizing the hierarchy, somehow, would still fail to solve the problem.

Roberts and Stephenson acknowledge that "there is evidence that Marx entertained the utopian concept of a planned hierarchy subject to democratic control, in which people's places in the hierarchy changed as often as four times a day," to which they cite Marx's passage in *The German Ideology*. But their attempt to reconcile radical democratic planning with what they believe must be highly centralized *hierarchical* planning may be forced. Indeed, the authors continue by saying "this would seem to be a planned and ordered society in which the hierarchical levels are of no social or political significance. They would merely be the organizational expression of the directly associated producers" (1973: 31), something that does not seem to accord very well with such an astute organizational theorist as Marx.

This, however, is just my point. They are not aware that this is an example of Marx's own struggle between workers' self-management and unified planning. They overlook that Marx's ideal of the praxis of planning is a utopian system of producers' and consumers' cooperatives linked through a general plan and social ownership. The producers and consumers as an overall group must, in their attempt to avoid an alienating hierarchy of knowledge, decide upon a comprehensive plan that rationally coordinates their production and consumption activities. This is the meaning of social ownership as opposed to state property, and participatory planning as opposed to command planning. Indeed, this utopian ideal is captured in the text of Yugoslavia's 1974 Constitution.[20]

SOCIAL PROPERTY AND THE IMAGINARY CONSTRUCTION
OF GENUINE CENTRAL PLANNING

Consider the common view of central planning as described in the theory of Soviet-style "command planning," which is to say, a system without market prices, hierarchically organized such that the whole of society is structured like a single firm with despotic, central administration. Michael Polanyi (1951) and Paul Craig Roberts (1971) have done an excellent and important job exposing the myth of central planning in the Soviet Union. They argue that material balances planning is a product of Soviet propaganda. It is not an economic reality. But Polanyi and Roberts have not influenced the greater part of the economics profession.[21] Nevertheless, for my immediate purpose we can consider the model not as an empirical description, but as a purely imaginary construction of genuine central planning and assess it from the Marxian view developed thus far.

The theory of material balances planning assumes that control over the economy's resources rests in a central planning bureau that oversees and directs all economic activity. It is said to operate in the following manner. Economic priorities, perhaps established by an exogenous agency, are given to the central planning bureau so it can plan a set of control figures and the inputs necessary to rationally achieve these figures. After the control figures are estimated, they are sent down the planning hierarchy to the individual administrative bodies. Each step along the way, the control figures become increasingly disaggregated into specific output targets for each industry and the enterprises which it comprises. After each enterprise reviews its own output target, it makes a specific statement or request for the inputs necessary to achieve the target. This information is then sent up the planning hierarchy, and becomes increasingly aggregated within the intermediary levels as a way of coordinating the needed inputs between enterprises in any given industry, and then between the various industries themselves. Bargaining at various levels acts as a correction principle to help alleviate apparent shortages or surpluses.

The goal is to achieve a material balance, an equality between supplies and demands of material inputs necessary to produce the targeted outputs. After an overall material balance has been achieved (we are now, once again, at the pinnacle of the planning hierarchy), the final targets and their material requirements then take the form of directives issued by the central planning board to the lower-order administrative bodies and enterprises within the planning hierarchy. Production then commences according to the plan.

Although this is supposed to rationally organize economic life, the political alienation which would result from such a bureaucracy is clear. The model does not recognize Marx's call for abolishing political alienation because the dualism between private and public life continues. In fact, only those at the top of the hierarchy, seated within the central planning board, fully participate in universal issues. The citizen, as producer, merely carries out the particular directives imposed by the hierarchy. The hierarchy of knowledge and total rule of the factory boss is universalized, not destroyed.

The pursuit of the Bolshevik ideal, and other efforts to centralize power, do tend to "make the whole of society as one office and one factory" (Lenin 1943: 84), and so reduce anarchic elements and may have paved the road to socialism by making organization more unified. It aspires to eliminate economic alienation stemming from anarchic market relations (as with Marx), but permits political alienation (contra Marx). Hence, achieving only hierarchical central planning is not enough for full-fledged Marxian socialism. That would retain, intensify, and universalize a power-politics alienation. What it leads to loses the other half of Marxism, and results in both political and economic alienation. Though people no longer confront the market as an alien will, they surely confront the central planning hierarchy as an alien power. As Marx says, the hierarchy itself is the principle abuse.[22]

The theory of material balances planning, or, indeed, any model that posits a planning system where full control rests within the central planning board, is inconsistent with the meaning of social ownership.

Marx has a well developed understanding of property rights and ownership. He is always quick to expose the contradiction between formal, legal rights and substantive rights. He recognizes, for example, that "the bureaucracy has the being of the state, the spiritual being of society, in its possession; it is its private property" (1970: 47), and he distinguishes between a legal claim and economic control:

a man may have a legal title to a thing without really having the thing. If, for instance, the income from a piece of land is lost owing to competition, then the proprietor has certainly the legal title to it along with the *jus utendi et abutendi* [right of using and consuming]. But he can do nothing with it: he owns nothing as a landed proprietor if in addition he has not enough capital to cultivate his ground. (Marx and Engels 1969, vol. 1: 79)

Marx recognizes that ownership implies control.[23] His notion of social ownership of the means of production implies that the control of economic resources rests in the community as a whole. Social ownership signifies a complex, indeed utopian, relationship whereby every relevant member of the community actively participates in the control of the community's resources. If it is to be more than a formal right, the power of disposal must rest concretely within the entire group of individuals who comprise the socialist community. The ideal of social ownership would point toward participatory, democratic planning through a system of producers' and consumers' councils.[24]

The imaginary construct of the centrally planned "command economy" by no means approaches the ideal of social ownership relations. In fact, if we consider ownership as the power of disposal, the command economy retains the institution of property. Although property may be legally defined as state property, or even social property, control over the factors of production, according to the model, stem from the individuals within the planning center alone. Those beneath the central planning board merely carry out the directives determined by and issued from the board, just as the worker carries out the directives issued from the capitalist boss.

The imaginary construct of a centrally planned economy, where control ultimately resides at the top of the hierarchy, may hypothetically eliminate market exchange. It does not eliminate property in the means of production. Instead, monopolized in a central planning board, property takes on its most concentrated, powerful form.

CONCLUSION

Economists who interpret the implications of Marx's critique of capitalism have generally examined the organizational side of Marx without paying close enough attention to the philosophical consequences. Informed by the praxis philosophical tradition, I have tried to show that the economic interpretation of Marx as a central planner seems misleading because central command planning clearly contradicts the radical humanistic goals of Marx's praxis program. Marx desired a radically decentralized, yet unified comprehensive plan.

Rather than interpreting Marx as a central planner, I maintain that it may be more worthwhile to interpret central planning as part of a struggle in Marx's own thinking. Struggles between humanistic decentralization and rationalistic centralization do not end with Marx. Tensions continue to haunt contemporary proposals for non-market as well as quasi-market socialism and workers' control.

In the next chapter I will have occasion to examine the other side of the tension. So far, I have concentrated largely upon the vision of socialism informed by praxis philosophy. In what follows I shall concentrate on the economics profession's account of worker-ownership and socialist economic organization. Informed especially by the arguments of Ludwig von Mises, F. A. Hayek, and Michael Polanyi, I shall proceed to critically examine the praxis philosophers' ideal of decentralized socialism from the perspective of rational economic organization.

NOTES

1. Marx surely erred. Certainly some classical economists used static analysis and ignored institutional development (David Ricardo, for instance, quickly comes

to mind). But others, such as Adam Smith and Thomas Malthus, offer a dynamic, evolutionary account of economic institutions. Marx's criticism seems more applicable to twentieth-century, neoclassical economics, whose nearly exclusive preoccupation with the properties of an abstract equilibrium has unfortunately slid the profession into irrelevancy. Many in the profession are now becoming increasingly aware of this "crisis in economic theory." See the papers in Bell and Kristol (1981) for a general overview of the crisis. Also see the more detailed and diverse criticisms in Caldwell (1982), Colander and Klamer (1987), High (1990), Kirzner (1986), Lavoie (1991), McCloskey (1985), O'Driscoll and Rizzo (1985), Samuels (1980), and Woo (1986). I have raised criticisms of neoclassical theory in Prychitko (1987; 1990c).

2. Karel Kosík makes this notion clear:

In the concept of praxis, socio-human reality is discovered as the opposite of givenness, i.e. at once as the process of forming human *being* and as its specific form. *Praxis* is the *sphere of human being*. In this sense, the concept of praxis is the outcome of *modern* philosophy which has emphasized, in a polemic against the Platono-Aristotelian tradition, the authentic character of man's creating, as of an ontological reality. Not only are existents "enriched" by man's work, but his work is where reality indeed manifests itself in a particular way and where access to it is negotiated. (1976: 136)

3. Agnes Heller says that Marx "establishes a norm against which we can measure the reality and value of our ideas, and with which we can determine the limitedness of our actions: it expresses the most beautiful aspiration of mature humanity, an aspiration that belongs to our being" (1988: 200).

4. "As a result, therefore, man (the worker) only feels himself freely active in his animal functions—eating, drinking, procreating, or at most in his dwelling and in dressing-up, etc.; and in his human functions he no longer feels himself to be anything but an animal" (1964: 111).

5. Cf. Marx's statements that run throughout his later work, *Capital*: "The persons exist for one another merely as representatives of, and, therefore, as owners of commodities. In the course of our investigation we shall find, in general, that the characters who appear on the economic stage are but the personification of the economic relations that exist between them" (1906: 97). When he addresses commodity fetishism, Marx writes: "There it is a definite social relationship between men, that assumes, in their eyes, the fantastic form of a relation between things" (1906: 83). Marx's underlying point is clear: people do not freely submit to estrangement. It must be forced upon them from without. But what is the exact source of estrangement? Marx, unfortunately, is ambiguous. Because he clearly states which aspects of capitalism are the consequences of estrangement, rather than its causes, however, we at least know what to exclude.

One probably expects that private property causes estrangement. It certainly contributes to estrangement in Marx's view. He argues, however: "though private property appears to be the source, the cause of alienated labor, it is rather its consequence, just as the gods are originally not the cause but the effect of man's intellectual confusion. Later this relationship becomes reciprocal" (1964: 117). Moreover, Marx maintains that every institution that spontaneously develops from private property—such as trade, competition, capital, and money—is "only a *definite* and *developed expression*" of estranged, alienated labor (p. 118).

6. Marx emphasizes that "the examination of *division of labor* and *exchange* is of extreme interest, because these are *perceptibly alienated* expressions of human activity and of *essential human power* as a *species* activity and power" (1964: 163).

7. See, for example, Marx (1906: 385-94). Wallimann (1981: 89-122) provides an exceptional account of Marx's view on the division of labor and its relationship to alienation.

8. Marx argues that the social division of labor appears before the development of market economies. Communities based predominantly upon tradition had a consciously planned and relatively simple social division of labor. Marx (1906: 49, 100) illustrates how the primitive Indian community, based on common property and barter, was organized by a social division of labor before the introduction of exchange and commodity production. Conscious control over the social division of labor is lost with the development of the commodity form: "The exchange of commodities . . . first begins on the boundaries of such communities, at their points of contact with other similar communities, or with members of the latter. So soon, however, as products once become commodities in their external relations of a community, they also, by reaction, become so in its internal intercourse" (p. 100). Hence, "the exchange of commodities breaks through all local and personal bounds inseparable from direct barter, and develops the circulation of the products of social labor; . . . it develops a whole network of social relations spontaneous in their growth and entirely beyond the control of the actors" (p. 126). The emergence of money and market exchange radically changes the character of the social division of labor, because it is no longer the product of our imagination. Rather, it appears to us as an alien will, according to Marx.

9. "The first metamorphosis of one commodity, its transformation from a commodity into money, is therefore also invariably the second metamorphosis of some other commodity, the retransformation of the latter from money into a commodity" (1906: 123).

10. More specifically, the capitalist hopes (though there is absolutely no guarantee) that the total cash revenues from the sale of the commodity will exceed that spent in its production. Hence, the capitalist plans to complete the following circuit: M—C—M', where M' = M + ΔM. If M' exceeds M the production of surplus value is demonstrated, for Marx.

11. Marx explains economic crises as the result of an overly long time interval between the purchase and sale of commodities, which leads to incorrect proportions between the supplies and demands of specific commodities. See Roberts and Stephenson (1973: ch. 4) for a good overview. Contemporary Marxian crisis theory has expanded to include the rationalizing and legitimating aspects of the capitalist welfare state, which, although now an apparatus expected to ward off economic crises, exacerbates if not initiates economic crises. See Habermas (1975) and Offe (1984).

12. For example, the leading economic historians of the Bolshevik Revolution in the USSR, such as Alexander Gerschenkron and Alec Nove, wish to deny the influence of Marx's vision on the Soviet experience. But that whole experience cannot be understood without an understanding of Marx's criticism of capitalism and his implicit vision of socialism. For a powerful critique of the standard economic history of the first decade of Soviet socialism, see Boettke (1990b).

13. Cf. Mihailo Marković (1974: 60): "Marx's key concepts invariably refer either

to structures which *are, but could be abolished*, or to those which *are not yet, but which could be created.*"

14. Although Marx's negative critique of capitalism implies a positive vision of socialism, the implicit vision must be one of fully developed socialism. Marx leaves it up to his followers to determine the difficult issue of how society goes from the here and now of capitalism to that future socialist ideal (see the fascinating studies by Boettke [1990b] and Polan [1984] on the problems Lenin and the Bolsheviks faced in their attempt to create socialism in the USSR). Marx's positive vision of socialism—the completely de-alienated society, where we all fulfill our human essence as praxis beings—comes after the "transition period," and those who read an implicit vision in Marx should not confuse that vision with the transition period itself—they are two logically distinct concepts. The former is concerned with the general characteristics of a fully developed socialist base (an *end-state*) while the latter is concerned with the transformation of the previous capitalist base toward a completely different base (a *process*). Surely interpretations of the end-state vision will color the process itself, but that does not justify equating the two.

15. Some disagree over the role of human nature in contemporary Marxism. The orthodox diamat philosophy jettisoned the notion of human nature in favor of a strict determinism between base and superstructure; and the structuralists (such as Althusser) dismiss the idea of transepochal human nature because, in their view, social structures are wildly different and therefore human nature must be incommensurable between structures. For an overview, see Marković's contribution on "Human Nature" in Bottomore et al. (1983: 214-17).

16. Roberts and Stephenson add that the "defining characteristic of Marxian socialism" is central planning (1973: 94). Lavoie writes that "there is implicit throughout Marx's writings a single, coherent, and remarkably consistent view of socialism" that culminates in central planning (1985c: 30).

17. Actually, in my view there is no way to achieve unity in a modern, technologically advanced economy, so even centralization is unworkable. That is, although the logical demands of rational non-market coordination may lead toward ever increasing centralization, the epistemological capacity required to fully plan a complex economy will fall short of that required for comprehensive planning. I shall discuss this knowledge problem in the next chapter.

18. It is also misleading to say that Marx believes alienation is a unique product of the developed market system. The developed market institutions of money, capitalist commodity production, and the spontaneously formed social division of labor are expressions of estranged labor, and estranged labor, according to Marx, appears long before commodity production becomes universalized into capitalist commodity production (1909, vol. 2: 43-44; 1964: 117).

19. Though rarely recognized as a methodological individualist, Marx nevertheless exposes the state (in contrast to Hegel's view) as an institution composed of social individuals: "He [Hegel] forgets that particular individuality is a human individual, and that the activities and agencies of the state are human activities . . . , nothing but the modes of existence and operation of the social qualities of men" (1970: 22). Or elsewhere: "The state is an abstraction; the people alone is the concrete" (p. 28).

20. See *The Constitution of the Socialist Federal Republic of Yugoslavia* Belgrade,

1974 (Ljubljana: Dopisna Delavska Univerza, n.d.), which I shall discuss in chapter 5.

21. There are some notable exceptions. Boettke (1990b) and Lavoie (1986–1987) have been directly influenced by the Polanyi-Roberts argument, as have I. Also see Powell (1977), Rutland (1985), and Zaleski (1980), whose arguments are similar to those of Roberts. The traditional view still prefers to model the Soviet system as a centrally planned command economy (cf., for example, Grossman 1963; Horvat 1982, chapter 2; Gregory and Stuart 1981). Comparative systems economists have developed a theoretical model of command planning that is thought to describe the so-called material balances planning of the USSR (cf., for example, Montias 1959). I shall discuss in the next chapter that the notion of material balances planning is very misleading if it is interpreted as an empirical description of the Soviet economy.

22. Similarly, Radoslav Selucký observes:

The producers do not work directly in order to produce use-values, but they work for entirely abstract and, in themselves, irrational plan targets. If Marx saw alienation of man from his work in the substitution of concrete labour by an abstract wage-earning activity, how would he view a situation in which the substitution of abstract activity for concrete labour persists and, on top of that, another intermediary has been interposed in the form of plan targets? In fact, nothing has changed for the better. The worker still works under the pressure of external necessity. He continues to be a *detail worker*. His labour continues to have meaning for him only as an abstract wage-earning activity. If, in the capitalist market system, his wage (exchange-value of his essential needs) was directly tied to the exchange-value of his product; now it is tied to it through plan targets. If, in the previous system, his work was alienated from him because he produced not directly for consumption but for the market, it is now alienated from him because he produces not directly for consumption but for the plan. (1979: 37-38)

23. Ludwig von Mises advanced a clear distinction between economic ownership and legal property rights in his 1922 book *Die Gemeinwirtschaft*, where he defines ownership as *control* over economic goods. Private property in the economic sense is "power of disposal" (Mises 1981b: 45). "Economically," Mises writes, "the natural *having* alone is relevant, and the economic significance of the legal *should have* lies only in the support that it lends to the acquisition, the maintenance, and the regaining of the natural *having*" (p. 27). Also see the more recent discussion by the Yugoslav economist Aleksandar Bajt: "Who the owner is in the economic sense is a question of fact: it is he who acquires benefit from the thing or, to use Marx's expression, he who appropriates" (Bajt 1968b: 152-53; cf. Bajt 1968a).

24. As Heller puts it:

At this point the following question arises: who makes the decisions about how productive capacity should be allocated? Who decides, for example, how long the production of goods directly serving consumption can "wait"? Marx's reply, of course, is *everyone* (this is precisely why he speaks of "associated individuals"). But how can every individual make such decisions? Marx did not answer this question, because for him it did not arise. For us, however, in our times, it has become perhaps the most decisive question of all. The focal point of contemporary Marxism is to work out models for this (or at least ought to be). (1988: 195-96)

André Gorz has also commented on the fundamentally utopian nature of praxis and its implications for social ownership and planning in Marx. He is worth quoting at length:

Its principal utopian content is that within it the proletariat is destined to realize the unity of the real as the unity of Reason: individuals divested of any individual interest as they are divested of any individual trade, are to unite universally in order to make their collaboration rational and voluntary and to produce together, in a single common praxis, a world which is totally theirs: nothing shall exist there independently of them. . . . The generalized self-management of material production is thus supposed to make redundant not only the separate apparatus of management, administration and co-ordination, but also the political sphere itself. The universal voluntary collaboration of "the united individuals" is supposed to be direct and transparent; it neither requires nor tolerates any mediation, for each individual "as total individual" assumes the whole totality of social production as her or his personal task. This task allows each to accede to the dignity of universal subject and total personal development through the development of all his or her faculties. (1989: 26-27)

CHAPTER 3 _____

Cooperation, Calculation, and Centralization: The Critique of Comprehensive Planning

I have argued that Marx was caught in an intellectual struggle. On the one hand he entertained a vision of praxis and the emancipation of economic and political alienation through a decentralized system of worker-managed cooperatives. On the other hand the elimination of commodity production and market exchange points toward centralized and hierarchical organization, which negates the praxis vision. Thus far I have placed more emphasis on Marx the praxis philosopher, and traced the decentralist socialist implications embedded within that perspective in order to challenge the Roberts-Stephenson-Lavoie view of Marxian socialism. In this chapter I shall have the opportunity to challenge the praxis interpretation of Marxian socialism by emphasizing the organizational logic that unfolds in the attempt to eliminate market exchange. In order to do so, I shall first focus on the history of the economics profession's analysis of producers' cooperatives and then continue on to one of the great debates in comparative economic systems, the problem of socialist calculation. Informed by the calculation argument, I shall then assess the praxis ideal of Marxian socialism.

ECONOMISTS ON COOPERATION

In 1848, in the midst of the debates over "utopian" and "scientific" systems of socialism, and in light of the many experiments in consumers' and producers' cooperatives and the attempts to establish integrated co-operative societies, the first edition of John Stuart Mill's *Principles of Political Economy* appeared. Published in seven editions during the author's lifetime, Mill's treatise became a standard textbook for generations of economists.

One gets the impression in the first edition of *Principles* that socialism (particularly in the writings of the French socialists, writings which Mill primarily concentrated upon) is largely undesirable and impractical, because it is unable to allocate labor efficiently without rivalrous markets. By the third edition (1852), Mill did encourage "an opportunity of trial" for the systems proposed by Saint-Simon and Fourier, but he nevertheless concluded that the political economist should not spend time envisioning new models and radical alternatives to capitalism. Only real world experience will determine the value of each system. "In the meantime," Mill remarked:

we may, without attempting to limit the ultimate capabilities of human nature, affirm, that the political economist, for a considerable time to come, will be chiefly concerned with the conditions of existence and progress belonging to a society founded on private property and individual competition; and that the object to be principally aimed at, in the present stage of human improvement, is not the subversion of the system of individual property, but the improvement of it, and the full participation of every member of the community in its benefits. (Mill 1926: 217)

Mill did focus on the development of the cooperative movement among the French working class, and concluded that the French experience "shows that the time is ripe for a larger and more rapid extension of association among labourers."[1]

The positive reforms brought about by the cooperative experiments impressed Mill to such an extent that, after considering practices of profit sharing and other capital-labor partnerships, he concluded:

The form of association, . . . which if mankind continue to improve, must be expected in the end to predominate, is not that which can exist between a capitalist as chief, and work-people without a voice in the management, but the association of the labourers themselves on terms of equality, collectively owning the capital with which they carry on their operations, and working under managers elected and removable by themselves. (pp. 772-73)

Mill believed cooperatives would prosper by directly competing with traditional capitalist firms. His reasons were straightforward: Because "individuals are more likely to commence things previously untried" (p. 791), the private capitalist is more willing to innovate. The manager of the cooperative organization could keep abreast of changing market conditions by being alert to the judgements and innovations of the capitalist. In this way market imitation "will be very useful in keeping the managers of co-operative societies up to the due pitch of activity and vigilance" (p. 791).

Mill contended that competition between cooperatives and capitalist enterprises may evolve ultimately into a system of cooperative societies because workers will no longer wish to work for wages, while capitalists, rather than hire the remaining "work-people of only the worst description," will instead loan their capital to cooperative enterprises. By the fifth edition (1862), Mill conclusively saw a "brilliant future reserved for the principle of co-operation" (1926: 782).

It was high time, then, that the economics profession began taking co-operation seriously. Indeed, by 1872 Henry Fawcett (a follower of Mill) echoed Mill's hope: "[cooperation's] general adaptation to industrial un-dertakings would probably mark the greatest advance ever yet made in human improvement. Labour and capital, instead of being hostile interests, will be united, and by this union an incalculable stimulus will be given to production" (1872: 13).[2] In his presidential address to the Twenty-first Annual Cooperative Congress (1889), the esteemed British economist Alfred Marshall glowed with optimism over the prospects of the cooper-ative movement, and regarded it "as the typical and most representative product of the age" (1889: 227).[3]

Meanwhile, in the United States debates raged over the prospects and possibilities of cooperation, instigated largely by F. A. Walker's critique. In *The Wages Question* (1876), Walker developed the concept of the en-trepreneur, a concept which was missing in the economic theory of distri-bution. The employer-entrepreneur, Walker reasoned, assumes the uncertainty of organizing labor of differing degrees of skill, combining labor with other scarce resources, and thereby producing a product . . . with no guarantee of its sale within the marketplace.[4] The employer-entrepreneur accordingly assumes the responsibilities of production and provides against contingencies, while using the faculties of technical skill, commercial knowledge, and the powers of administration (Walker 1968: 244-45).[5]

Walker reacted against Mill's belief that cooperation would replace the "mere distributors, who are not producers but auxiliaries of production" (Mill 1926: 789) and thereby lead to ever greater efficiencies in production and distribution. Recognizing that entrepreneurial ability is a scarce human faculty, Walker argued to the contrary: producers' cooperation, "consid-ered as a question in the distribution of wealth, is nothing more or less than getting rid of the employer, the entrepreneur, the middleman. It does not get rid of the capitalist." Walker maintained that the cooperative must combine "in the same person, not the labor function and capital function, but the labor function and the entrepreneur function" (1968: 265; cf. 1892: 213-14). Because entrepreneurial ability is scarce, Walker concluded there is little likelihood of successful, lasting producers' cooperation.[6]

Walker's pessimism did not, however, convince Richard T. Ely and his associates. Ely, whom Schumpeter describes as "that excellent German professor in American skin" (1954: 874, n. 19), was devoted to historical analysis and social change (although he leaned, perhaps, toward outright historicism), and was enamored with the labor movement in the United States, particularly with the apparent success of producer cooperation within the cooperage industry in Minneapolis.[7] During this period, the 1880s, the cooperative movement had in fact expanded very rapidly in the United States,[8] and the promise of producers' cooperation became the hot topic of the day among progressive-minded members of the American economics profession.[9]

Ely and his colleagues interpreted the labor movement's turn toward cooperation as an attempt to establish a new social order. Ely fought against claims that cooperation "merely means business." "If that is all," Ely quipped, "let us turn our attention to some more profitable and interesting topic." For Ely there was much more to the cooperative movement than everyday business. Indeed, he heralded the cooperative movement as "a complete, though peaceful, transformation of society" (Ely 1969: 169; cf. 1886: 7, 1887: 151). Linking the movement to his Christian faith, Ely claimed that cooperation "alone is compatible with the ultimate complete triumph for Christianity" (1887: 151).[10]

Other American economists argued that cooperation was, at best, a very limited form of industrial organization. John Bates Clark (1967: 175-96), for example, argued that cooperation should have a fair chance to coexist in a competitive environment, but he did not believe the cooperative format could be universally applied to all business organizations. Others, such as Edwin R. A. Seligman, reiterated Walker's argument regarding the scarcity of entrepreneurial ability in the common working person. Arthur T. Hadley went to extremes by claiming that the industries of his day "must have efficient leadership and unquestioned authority—one man power" (see Barns 1971: 55, 63).

Moreover, many cooperative ventures went out of business or collapsed into *de facto* joint stock companies. Most of the cooperatives established during the 1860s, 70s, and 80s had succumbed by the 1890s.[11] But many of the cooperatives were developed in response to short-run exigencies that resulted from rapid changes in labor market conditions.[12] Others failed as a result of either bad business skills or because they had been formed to protect skills which were rapidly being replaced by mechanization and the realization of economies of scale. Moreover, and perhaps more importantly, it seems that the growing consciousness of the Progressive Era, with its optimistic call for large-scale, organized labor unionism, trusts, and industrial partnerships, eclipsed the expected value of producers' cooperation.

Richard Ely and his associates began to retreat from their defense of producers' cooperatives by the turn of the century. By 1903, Ely had outlined a "scientific alternative of socialism" that included private property, competition and its regulation by government, the necessity of public municipalities, and state welfare programs to ensure a more equitable distribution of wealth. The call for producers' cooperatives is conspicuously absent (Ely 1971, vol. 2: 468-69).[13] "The true ideal" for Ely now lay "midway between anarchy and socialism, and may be termed the principle of social solidarity." Replacing the cooperative principle with that of social solidarity, Ely maintained that "the great institutions of society must be conserved, but developed in the interests of liberty positively conceived. There must be a carefully elaborated and widely executed regulation of economic relations" (pp. 421-22).

The notion of cooperation had changed its meaning well beyond that of experiments in consumers' and producers' cooperatives. Now it meant the organization of labor, business and government interests under the form of state regulation of competition, the promotion of trusts, partnerships, and public municipalities. The call for industrial reform beyond producers' cooperation had been growing, of course, during the late 1800s. Henry C. Adams, for instance, argued that trusts and industrial partnerships were a better means of industrial reform than producers' cooperation, which, though "good enough in its own way," "as a practical solution to the labor problem . . . counts for little" (Adams quoted in Barns 1971: 63). Hope lay more in the form of state regulation and planning.[14]

THE RISE OF SCIENTIFIC MANAGEMENT AND CENTRAL PLANNING

Other currents contributed to the economics profession's turn from the traditional notion of producers' cooperation. Not only had the apparent failure of producers' cooperatives, and the newly found hope in the cartelization of industry, caused the shift of focus. A more subtle, philosophical undercurrent had gained momentum within business practice and the social sciences. Philosophical positivism produced the ideology of scientific management.[15]

Scientific management surfaced with the publication of Henry R. Towne's "The Engineer as an Economist" (1886), a paper he delivered to the American Society of Mechanical Engineers (ASME). Though sketchy, Towne's general message encouraged the link between workplace organization and engineering (particularly mechanical engineering), for "the matter of shop management is of equal importance with that of engineering" (1886: 48). But it was Towne's rival, Frederick Winslow Taylor, whose 1895 lecture "A Piece Rate System, being a step toward a Partial Solution of the Labor Problem" (also delivered to the ASME) developed more fully the notion of scientific management, and had soon acquired the label "Taylorism."[16]

Taylor, like other science- and efficiency-minded intellectuals of the time, was motivated by the need to "solve" the "labor problem" (the "soldiering" of the workforce—the unionization of working people and the subsequent strike activities that followed). He sought a "complete re-division of the work" within the shop, such that work would be "divided into two large sections," whereby "one of those sections is handed over to the management" (Taylor 1916: 75). Although Taylor could not resist using the "cooperation" slogan ("It represents a democracy, co-operation, a genuine division of work which never existed before in this world" [pp. 75-76]), it is clear that this approach to business organization expunged the possibility of meaningful producers' cooperation (which, of course, did not concern Taylor at all). Scientific management meant "Taking the control of the machine shop out of the hands of the many workmen, and placing it completely in the hands of the management, thus superseding the 'rule of thumb' by scientific control" (Taylor quoted in Sohn-Rethel 1978: 152).

Under scientific management, "the workman is told minutely just what he is to do and how he is to do it; and any improvement which he makes upon the orders given him is fatal to success" (Taylor quoted in Sohn-Rethel 1978: 152). In the scientifically managed workshop, "Every little trifle,—there is nothing too small,—becomes the subject of experiment. The experiments develop into a law" (Taylor 1916: 75).[17]

By 1908, the new Harvard Business School adopted Taylorism as the "foundation concept" of modern management, and by 1910 Louis Brandeis (in his famous Eastern Rate Case testimony) vigorously argued for applied scientific management: he maintained that the Santa Fe Railroad did not need a rate increase it was pleading for, because it could "save a million dollars a day" by imposing scientific management principles. Scientific management had quickly become entrenched in American business practice.[18]

Scientific management also garnered widespread support outside the United States. While Taylor restricted his analysis to small workshops, others claimed that scientific management could be used to rationalize any form of organization.[19] After all, if a capitalist factory could increase its efficiency through a unified, central plan that makes workers subservient to an authoritative boss and uses incentive schemes calculated to maximize output, what stops this method from applying to any organization? The German state, for example, adopted scientific management practices to mobilize forces for the First World War. As Judith Merkle points out, "Successful militarism not only elevated cultural values of commandism, but required the development of thought about both systematic organization for planning, and for the arrangement of logistical support" (1980: 175). Scientific management filled this role. In fact, scientific management evolved from the notion of workshop organization to nothing short of a political philosophy, as expressed by the philosopher-industrialist Walther Rathenau and the mechanical engineer Richard von Moellondorff (see Merkle 1980: 172-207).

The German war economy became an exemplary model of economic efficiency. Ironically, progressives considered the war planning model a useful tool for peacetime management of economies as well (cf. Hayek 1975: 29-32). As Wesley C. Mitchell said in May 1918, "it seems impossible that the countries concerned will attempt to solve [the new contingencies peace would bring] without utilizing the same sort of centralized direction now employed to kill their enemies abroad for the new purpose of reconstructing their own life at home," for "The war has demonstrated the feasibility of considerable and rapid changes under the pressure of circumstances" (quoted in Dorfman 1969, vol. 3: 490).[20] Later, John Maurice Clark (the son of J. B. Clark) similarly appealed to national economic planning on the basis of the experience during the First World War, and pointed to the virtues of scientific management. He argued:

In the past, most observers felt that central control could not do better than unplanned competition; and they focused their attention on the marvelous fact that free exchange without central planning does produce some sort of order. This may have been the proper attitude at the time, in view of the prevailing ignorance of the principles of large-scale organization, and of the nature of the problem of business depression. But it is not a proper attitude now. (Clark 1967: 240)

The German war economy also influenced Lenin in Bolshevik Russia so much that he revised his Marxist criticisms of Taylorism (though he did not adopt it completely):

Now that the workers, and no longer the bourgeoisie, hold power, we cannot reject Taylorism wholesale. Instead, we must remove its bourgeois trappings with the help of scientific research and practical experience and examine it carefully for those elements which could facilitate the work process and offer some relief to the worker by transferring the hard physical labor to the machine. Only in this way can we reach the state where the worker only had to adjust the heavy machinery; consequently, general productivity in the factory can be increased. (Lenin quoted in Traub 1978: 84; cf. Lenin 1914)

By 1921 the Bolsheviks had empowered twenty institutes to formulate and apply scientific management, with Moscow's Central Institute of Labor as the major organization of this kind. Created in 1920, and directed by Alexej Kapitonovich Gastev, it had as its purpose the promotion of scientific management in all walks of life: it called for nothing less than complete "social engineering." This approach did not seem to fare well with Marx's vision of praxis, and Gastev's apologetics seemed weak, unconvincing, and alienating: "Many find it repugnant that we want to deal with human beings as with a screw, a nut, a machine. But we must undertake this as fearlessly as we accept the growth of trees and the expansion of the railway network" (Gastev quoted in Traub 1978: 87-89).[21]

In the midst of the Bolshevik Revolution, Lenin, influenced by the organizational side of Marx, envisaged turning "the whole of society" into "one office and one factory." Nikolai Bukharin claimed that this organization would consist ideally of a system of "cooperative" organs, but it would nevertheless be subject to a centrally unified economic plan imposed by the authority of the proletarian state. Bukharin stressed that "one of the fundamental tasks of the Soviet Power was and is that of uniting all the economic activities of the country in accordance with a general plan of direction by the State" (Bukharin and Preobrazhensky 1966: 266). The Supreme Economic Council would be entrusted with the responsibility to coordinate "all economic activities of the country," by attempting to "draw up and to carry out a unified scheme for the State administration of economic life" (p. 269). Abolishing the anarchy of capitalist production meant, in turn, erecting a "great united, organized, 'mechanized' system of social production" (p. 277).

Interest in traditional producers' cooperation declined, both in theory and practice. As Harry W. Laidler put it: "The World War came. Revolution followed. Communism loomed up in the East, and the communist or bolshevik philosophy began to command the attention of the world as a new and potent phase of revolutionary thinking" (1927: 681). Economists began to concentrate upon comparative systems of economic organization. As opposed to cooperative production per se, the profession began to think more systematically about the notions of centrally planned versus market allocated systems. The debate over the possibility of economic calculation under socialism was just on the horizon.

CENTRAL PLANNING AND THE SOCIALIST CALCULATION DEBATE

The question over whether socialism is feasible led to one of the great debates within the economics profession during the interwar period. Ludwig von Mises's 1920 statement, "Economic Calculation in the Socialist Commonwealth," ignited a controversy that engaged the profession for two decades. And in many ways the debate has not ended.[22]

Mises understood socialism to be an economic system that, having abolished the capitalist institutions of private property, money, and commodity production, would in turn coordinate economic activities under the authority of a central planning board. The goal of German Marxism at the time was to overthrow the market (an *ex post* coordinator of economic activities) for an *ex ante* coordinator of economic activities—a general plan scientifically designed and executed from a single controlling center. With this understanding in mind, Mises issued the following challenge: Upon what basis would the central planning board rationally calculate the scarcities of economic goods?

Mises, the leading figure within the Austrian School of economics during the 1920s, had been influenced by Eugen Boehm-Bawerk's earlier critique of Marx's labor theory of value (see the exchange between Boehm-Bawerk and Hilferding in Sweezy 1975), and hence Mises did not consider the Marxian labor time analysis a solution to rational central planning.[23] Instead, Mises focused his critique on the knowledge provided by spontaneously generated market prices.

Mises argued that unhampered market prices act as "aids to the mind" under the anarchic organization of capitalist industry. Market prices allow individual enterprises to judge the economic efficiency of their activities by using profit and loss accounting. Though neither perfect nor universally applicable to all valued goods, monetary calculation is indispensable for coordinating intricately connected production processes. Mises maintained that an advanced economic system owes its complexity to monetary calculation, and could not continue to grow without relying upon profit-loss calculations reckoned according to spontaneously formed market prices.

Because socialism seeks to replace private ownership of the means of production with state or social ownership, capital goods would cease being objects of exchange—the market for capital goods would be abolished. Without these markets, Mises maintained, scarcity indicating prices for the means of production would be abolished. And without these prices, he concluded, rational economic planning is impossible.

Mises claimed that unhampered market exchange supplies knowledge to the social actors in the economy. Central planning, which seeks to destroy the anarchy of production, cannot rationally allocate scarce economic resources because the central planning board simply does not have the requisite knowledge to do so. As Mises said, "No single man can ever master all the possibilities of production, innumerable as they are, as to be in a position to make straightway evident judgements of value without the aid of some system of computation" (Mises 1920: 102). For Mises, such a system requires market prices.[24]

Mises's essay was translated into English in 1935, and his *Die Gemeinwirtschaft* was translated as *Socialism* in 1936. Later that year, Oskar Lange attempted to disprove Mises's argument that rational economic calculation under socialism is impossible (Lange 1936).

Lange had borrowed some key ideas developed earlier by Enrico Barone and Fred M. Taylor. In "The Ministry of Production in the Collectivist State," Barone (1908) had argued that both capitalism and socialism must solve a similar problem: each system must efficiently allocate scarce resources. Barone demonstrated the theoretical possibility of socialism by working with simultaneous equations within an abstract, general equilibrium framework. He argued that either system can reach a determinate equilibrium solution by solving a system of simultaneous equations, as long as the number of independent equations equals the number of unknowns. Either system must solve the same set of equations. In principle, the system is solved by the market under capitalism, and by central planning under socialism. But Barone also maintained that, although we may know what the structure of the equations looks like, the central planning board will not be able to solve the system because there are simply too many equations—millions of them, in fact.

Barone concluded that although capitalism and socialism are formally similar (that is, they both face the same economic problem), capitalism offers a better chance of actually solving the equations, and therefore achieving equilibrium.[25] In his presidential address to the American Economic Association, Fred M. Taylor (1929) added that the market indeed "solves" this system of equations, but it does so by "trial and error." Market prices tend to equilibrate supplies and demands due to the guesswork on behalf of independent producers and consumers.

Lange combined Barone's formal approach with Taylor's trial-and-error explanation in his attempt to answer Mises. In Lange's model, the central planning board must first determine the prices of consumer goods (which would then be used to impute value to higher order, capital goods). The central planning board proceeds by establishing some initial set of prices. Chances are that the initial prices will not be equilibrium prices—as evidenced by shortages and surpluses. A price above equilibrium results in a rising inventory of consumer goods. This sends a signal to the planners to lower the price; likewise, a price initially set below equilibrium results in a falling inventory, and thus alerts the planners to raise the price. Lange claimed that, through trial and error, the central planning board could effectively establish the equilibrium set of prices. In fact, he believed the central planning board could do so more quickly and with less error than the market does with millions of independent competing entrepreneurs:

Indeed, it seems that this trial and error procedure would, or at least could, work *much better* in a socialist economy than it does in a competitive market. For the Central Planning Board has a much wider knowledge of what is going on in the whole economic system than any private entrepreneur can ever have, and, consequently, may be able to reach the right equilibrium prices by a *much shorter* series of successive trials than a competitive market actually does. (Lange 1936: 89)[26]

And, by constraining the socialist enterprises to (1) produce a level of output where price equals marginal cost (price being determined by the central planning board and taken as a parameter by the enterprises) and

(2) to minimize the average total cost of production, market socialism would mirror the efficiency conditions that perfectly competitive capitalism hypothetically achieves.

Lange impressively answers the issue of computing the equations modeled by Barone. Indeed, he should convince standard neoclassical economists of the possibility of rational calculation under socialism: if neoclassical economists explain market coordination by way of the *tatonnement* process of the Walrasian auctioneer, then it seems reasonable that a central planning board could replace the auctioneer, in theory.[27]

Lange did not, however, answer Mises's argument. Nor did Mises's colleagues—F. A. Hayek and Lionel Robbins—retreat from Mises's impossibility argument, as the standard account of the socialist calculation debate suggests. True, Hayek (1975: 207) had indeed said "it must be admitted that this [the abstract mathematical solution] is not an impossibility in the sense that it is logically contradictory," and Robbins responded that "we can conceive this problem to be solved by a series of mathematical calculations" but "in practice this solution is quite unworkable" because it would necessitate compiling and solving "millions of equations" (1934: 151). But their statements did not constitute a "retreat" from the Misesian position (and hence imply that Mises was wrong), as Lange erroneously claimed (1936: 63).[28] Mises maintained from the beginning that the problem of economic calculation is not an issue in static economic theory. Rather, it is a practical problem of dynamic, everyday economics.[29]

Don Lavoie, in his detailed study of the debate, argues that the profession's general acceptance of the Lange position misdirected the debate. The socialist calculation debate began with questions about economic calculation under real world conditions of change, uncertainty, and scarcity, but was "answered" by resorting to the statics of pure, institutionless economic theory (1985c: 78-144). Mises's contention was not proven wrong. It was recast in a neoclassical, equilibrium framework and consequently misunderstood. Mises and Hayek considered the fundamental problem to be one of formulating or determining the "equations" of the economic system, as it were, rather than computing a given set of equations. They had maintained that, in the endlessly changing, uncertain world of everyday life, the central planners would lack the requisite knowledge to determine the "coefficients" that make up the "equations," because this knowledge is spread across all the agents that compose the economic system, and cannot be aggregated or concentrated in any form useful for the central planning board. Although one may theoretically demonstrate that a solution can be found by computing a given set of simultaneous equations, the issue of real-world socialist calculation nevertheless remains one of formulating the "equations" themselves (to keep within the language of general equilibrium theory).

Both sides, however, consider themselves winners of the debate. Lange and his followers have shown that, in the neoclassical fiction of general equilibrium, socialist calculation is rational as long as a market for consumer goods is present, which imputes values to higher order capital goods. Mises and the Austrians believe they have won, because Lange and his adherents were forced to adopt at least a quasi-market for socialist allocation, and, more importantly, because they still failed to demonstrate how rational economic calculation would be possible in a complex, dynamic system.

Much of this confusion stems from the fact that the Austrians did not clearly distinguish themselves from the neoclassical mainstream. Their views of the nature of economic science, the use of equilibrium constructs, the meaning of competition and market-generated prices, etc. differed remarkably from the mainstream.[30] As Karen Vaughn remarks, those in favor of socialism (with the exception of Maurice Dobb)

took their inspiration from Marshall, more from Walras, but all agreed that given some "just" initial wealth distribution, equilibrium in the perfectly competitive model represented the maximization of human welfare, and all their programs for socialism were designed to reproduce the conclusions of perfect competition in a centrally directed economy.

While the Austrians, who viewed competition as a rivalrous process rather than an equilibrium end-state,

worked with a perception of economic activity that differed markedly from that [of] mainstream economists. Primarily, they questioned the relevance and applicability of static equilibrium models in which all information is given, and emphasized instead the process by which decentralized economic actors operating in a world of uncertainty and constant change [would] bring about the coordination of production and consumption plans. (Vaughn 1980b: 536-37)

Unfortunately, these differences were misunderstood by the participants in the debate. The Austrians are partly to blame here, because in their zeal to expose the shortcomings of the labor theory of value (particularly its Marxist variant), they mistakenly aligned themselves with the neoclassical exponents of marginal value theory. As Lavoie writes:

A more critical attitude toward the neoclassical approach early in the debate could have prevented much of the confusion that developed later on. The early Austrian theorists were too eager, in my view, to embrace neoclassical economists as marginalist allies against the threat of resurgent classical value theory in the form of Marxism. This kept them from realizing that on some issues they and the Marxists had more in common than either did with the sort of neoclassical economics that underlies the market socialist proposals. (1985c: 3)

Neither side realized the extent to which they were debating across incommensurable paradigms of thought. Not only was misunderstanding inevitable, but, as Vaughn states, the socialist calculation debate was ultimately "a contest of theoretical models in which a mutually satisfactory resolution was precluded from the outset" (Vaughn 1980b: 537).

TOTALITARIAN CENTRALIZATION: THE LOGIC OF COMPREHENSIVE PLANNING

The Bolsheviks' attempt to centrally plan the economy during the War Communism period in Soviet history (1918-1921) was taken by the Austrians as evidence of their argument. During War Communism, enterprises were nationalized, while market exchange and money were abolished. The ensuing economic calamity that had resulted demonstrated Mises's point that central planning must necessarily be irrational. Hence, the Bolsheviks were forced to submit to market-based allocation as legitimized under the New Economic Policy. Later, in the 1930s and 1940s, Lange and his followers considered Stalin's Five Year Plans to be evidence that central planning works in practice (that Stalin's model had nothing in common with Lange's seemed to be beside the point).

During the post-war era that followed the socialist calculation debate, F. A. Hayek turned his attention to the totalitarian nature of so-called centrally planned economies in his *The Road to Serfdom* (1944). His message was strong and uncompromising: "Planning leads to dictatorship," Hayek claimed, "because dictatorship is the most effective instrument of coercion and the enforcement of ideals and, as such, essential if central planning on a large scale is to be possible" (p. 70). Hayek had not admitted that central planning was possible in practice. Rather, he traced the *logical* consequences that unfold during the attempt to replace market organization with comprehensive planning.[31]

Hayek advanced the classical liberal thesis that political freedom cannot be had without economic freedom, regardless of the moral aspirations of the planning body. In a world of scarcity, economic planning necessarily entails choosing between conflicting ends. To develop a unified economic plan means some individuals' ends must be sacrificed for the satisfaction of others; that choice cannot be left to the spontaneous actions of individual agents within the system, for this is precisely the "anarchic" feature of markets that Marx finds alienating in the economic sense. Opposed to the rivalry between a multitude of individuals, the central planning board must attempt to allocate systematically scarce resources for the benefit of society as a whole. Otherwise only chaos would result. And it will attempt to do so in a scientifically organized, detailed plan. Hayek maintains that if the economic goal of socialism is the elimination of the uncontrolled anarchy of the market process through the rationally planned organization of economic activity, some disturbing political consequences logically follow.

Because the central planning board attempts to control economic activity rationally, the board must bring under its control the means individuals use to satisfy their ends. This necessarily implies that the board must also determine which *ends* are worthy of social pursuit. "Economic control is not merely control of a sector of human life which can be separated from the rest," Hayek argues. Instead, "it is the control of the means for all our ends" (p. 92). The discretion over which ends will be pursued and which will be foregone must rest squarely within a central planning board.

The maintenance and well-being of society depends upon the workings of a smoothly functioning, rational plan. But the planning board would face an immeasurable degree of complexity when it tries to develop a feasible plan of action. Without a system of market prices to serve as a means to convey and use the knowledge required to coordinate the economic activities of the participants within the system, the planners will find that the task they confront will be constrained more by epistemological limitations than by moral principles. That is, though they may believe they possess objective guidelines of economic justice (to each according to his needs, from each according to his abilities, all the power to the soviets, and so forth, down to the most minute details), they will soon face an obstacle when it comes to fulfilling their goals of justice. They will inevitably lack useful criteria to guide them in acquiring and transmitting the detailed and relevant knowledge that is necessary to comprehensively coordinate the system. The planning apparatus, in its sincere attempt to seek a unified plan, must make its task more manageable by restricting the role of voluntary agreement and democratic influence. Hayek writes:

An economic plan, to deserve the name, must have a unitary conception. Even if a parliament could, proceeding step by step, agree on some scheme, it would certainly in the end satisfy nobody. A complex whole in which all the parts must be most carefully adjusted to each other cannot be achieved through a compromise between conflicting views. To draw up an economic plan in this fashion is even less possible than, for example, successfully to plan a military campaign by democratic procedure. As in strategy it would become inevitable to delegate the task to experts. (p. 64)

Consequently, even if the ideal is a fully participatory form of comprehensive planning (as opposed to a purely centralized regime), the planning board will not submit to democratic means, for it will soon find that it cannot place socially important technical issues into the hands of society as a whole. Rather, the planning board will deem it necessary, if rationalized production, distribution, and consumption activities are to ever commence, to pursue those social ends that *it* deems technically possible and economically and socially worthwhile:

That the complex system of interrelated activities, if it is to be consciously directed at all, must be directed by a staff of experts, and that ultimate responsibility and power must rest in the hands of a commander-in-chief whose actions must not be fettered by democratic procedure, is too obvious a consequence of underlying ideas of central planning not to command fairly general assent. (p. 88)

The organizational logic of planning presents the major problem. The knowledge problem of socialism gives rise to a totalitarian problem as well. The planning board must assume a monopoly of control over production. It alone must enjoy the power to override the desires of those it claims to represent. By overthrowing the fetters of democratic decision-making,

it would have complete power to decide what we are to be given and on what terms. It would not only decide what commodities and services were to be available and in what quantities; it would be able to direct their distribution between districts and groups and could, if it wished, discriminate between persons to any degree it liked. If we remember why planning is advocated by most people, can there be much doubt that this power would be used for the ends of which the authority approves and to prevent the pursuits of ends which it disapproves? (p. 93)

Society will therefore be divided into those who do the planning, and those whose life activities are planned from the outside. Alienation appears once again. Though one may hope that the planners are morally enlightened and humane people, Hayek argues that there is good reason to believe that only "the worst get on top," because, in its attempt to concentrate power in order to execute a unified plan, the central planning board must also demand unquestioned allegiance by the masses. It must ensure that the planners' goals are thought to be those of society as a whole. As such, the centrally planned society becomes politicized (in the sense of politics as the embodiment of coercive power and force), and the potential for politics as a rational dialogue between social individuals concerning their rights and responsibilities must necessarily cease to exist. In its quest for truth, genuine political dialogue implies the freedom to challenge, to be critical, and to dissent. The central planning board, however, cannot help but exploit its monopoly over the production process by putting an end to social criticism, because criticism, and the unintended consequences it must yield, necessarily acts as a fetter upon the conscious organization of society. In the end, propaganda must replace any potential for authentic political dialogue.

Hayek deduces the organizational consequences that appear in the attempt to eliminate the market. He assumes that the planners sincerely wish to organize society rationally for the betterment of its citizens. Others have argued that existing Soviet-style systems, failing to completely abolish the anarchy of market relationships with a comprehensive plan, have instead erected a myth of the plan. Soviet Five Year Plans do not provide evidence that central planning works. Rather, they were an ideological facade constructed to legitimize the all-powerful Soviet state.

The Soviet economy was not planned from a single center. Even before its present push toward *perestroika*, the Soviet system had been "polycentrically" planned, as Michael Polanyi, the Hungarian scientist and philosopher, argued. Polanyi maintained that the Soviet system offered at best the illusion of being integrally and rationally planned from the center. Material balances planning was as much a myth in Soviet and East European economies as the model of perfect competition is in Western capitalist economies.

In practice, the system's complexity necessarily overwhelmed those who appeared to be directing the economy, as Hayek suggests. Rather than an unambiguous directive issued from the higher levels of the planning hierarchy, the individual enterprise managers received a plethora of often contradictory directives. In order to "fulfill the plan," then, each socialist enterprise manager relied primarily upon his own judgement and selected that "directive" which he considered most rational for achieving the ends of the enterprise he represented (these ends may be economic or political).

The problem here is clear. If one chooses a directive, then it is really not a directive at all. As Polanyi (1951: 111-37, 154-200) and Paul Craig Roberts (1971: 70-88) have shown, coordination took place at the disaggregated level, among individual enterprises that coordinate their plans in anarchic black market exchanges of scarce capital goods. The economic system is thus best described as polycentrically coordinated as opposed to centrally planned. It does not differ in kind from the commodity production-relations of capitalism, for the fundamental organizing principle—anarchic exchange—has not been overcome. Though the quantity and quality of outputs chosen and produced at each individual enterprise level had become aggregated into a so-called central plan, and indeed would later be published as a unified, centrally issued plan established by the directives of the Soviet state, in fact the coordination of economic activities took place at the enterprise level, at the bottom of the hierarchy. Those at the top of the hierarchy enjoyed an unparalleled degree of political power, but they did not possess any meaningful degree of rational economic control over the coordination process, nor could they understand it in any degree of detail (see Lavoie 1986-1987: 11-15).[32]

Hayek's original argument in *The Road to Serfdom* seems to go a long way toward explaining the totalitarian, centralizing tendencies that have developed in "real existing socialism." It also confirms that the Marxian vision of a completely decentralized and fully participatory socialism is an impossible utopia. Unfortunately, the praxis philosophers who have supported this vision apparently believe that the totalitarian problem is a separate issue of the transition period, rather than an unintended result of trying to abolish the system of anarchic market exchange.

THE TOTALITARIAN PROBLEM AMONG PRAXIS
PHILOSOPHERS

During the transition from capitalism to socialism, says Mihailo Marković,

the critical question is will this elite ... find within itself the moral strength and consistency to pass voluntarily to the basic element of the socialist revolution? (i.e., to the realization of self-government, and consequently the gradual setting aside of itself as a powerful elite.). ... Or will several decades of intense concentration of power in its hands so change its nature that this elite will identify itself with socialism and will want to cling permanently to its political and material privileges, and will want to remain permanently not only the mind but the iron hand of progress? (1982: 25)

Marković asks how the socialist revolution will bring about the political freedoms envisioned by Marx. He notes that the political sphere in contemporary capitalist systems lacks a significantly dialogical foundation (indeed, have we ever enjoyed the possibility of a generalized, uncoerced dialogue?) and hence has "missed the real possibilities of an authentic, rich life." Moreover, the so-called centrally planned economies have (as Hayek suggests in principle) intensified the problem, for there is "an even greater tendency ... to concentrate the majority of decisions concerning all key social questions in the hands of a limited group of rulers" (pp. 25-26). In a world of dehumanizing and nearly unlimited state power, Marković and other Yugoslav praxis philosophers traditionally maintained that the state's attempt to centrally plan an economy is itself a fundamental vehicle of alienation. As Pedrag Vranicki writes, "The only difference in this instance is that capitalist monopoly has been supplanted by the universal monopoly of the state" (1965: 306).

While the Praxis group seems to believe the myth of central planning in the Soviet state,[33] Zagorka Golubović comes closest, however, to piercing the veil of socialist central planning. For example, she writes:

When socialist goals were converted into national objectives, the criteria for evaluating progress became more discernable: national prosperity was measured against the visible material progress of capitalist countries. The *language of figures* came into usage in order to prove the great advantage of a "socialist way" of development over the capitalist. Naturally, within this framework it was not possible to employ as "facts" either the development of revolutionary power, the transformation of inter-personal relations, or a greater degree of freedom to serve as the "unit for measuring progress." Per capita production of steel, electrical energy, and so forth, served instead as the appropriate unit of measure. This approach to development upheld the "necessity for strengthening the state in socialism." (1981: 133; emphasis added)

Polanyi, Roberts, Lavoie, and others who hold to the myth of the plan thesis argue that this "language of figures" is all that there is to the "plan." These "facts" of economic "development," articulated and published by the bureaus within the planning hierarchy, are strung together in order to legitimate and further strengthen state power.

The Soviets, according to Golubović, have created another myth: the myth of the "leading role of the working class" (p. 133). Abolishing the bourgeois state, only to replace it with an equally if not more oppressive socialist state, clearly fails to solve the problem of freedom in Marx's sense. In a point that echoes Hayek, Golubović argues that in such a system "Only the ruling class possesses all means necessary for establishing class identity and for leading class struggles, including means of repression. All other classes cannot express themselves as a class or defend their interests since they have neither their own organizations nor are allowed to develop their own ideology" (p. 133).

Marković (1982: 29-31) summarizes the contemporary praxis critique of alienation under bureaucracy (alienation which develops under capitalism and is intensified under statism) with the following points.

Alienation arises through the professionalization of politics. Politics and political ideas become commodified. Politics becomes a source of income and power, a career rather than an arena of open dialogue in the community's search for ethical truths and a sense of identity. This criticism stems from Jürgen Habermas's argument that politics has become infused with instrumental reason—philosophical positivism promotes a "scientization of politics" whereby the ends of social life fall outside the sphere of rational discourse. Value systems (questions and claims about the good life, about what should be done) are shaped by technical possibilities and the apparently optimal means by which to achieve them. Insulated from critical reflection, values have become strictly conservative. Professional politics assumes a social engineering mentality; it becomes simply the technical means by which to achieve a given (generally unquestioned) set of goals (Habermas 1970: 62-80).

This leads to Marković's second point. Agents of the state treat the majority of their constituents as mere objects—things—in order to achieve their own agendas. "This is the highest and most subtle form of reification," Marković claims, because "never have so many people been so successfully manipulated, thanks, among other things, to the extraordinary technical perfection of all forms of propaganda" (1982: 30). Along with reification, the state also embodies another destructive force—exploitation. As the state grows, and increases its power over issues of distribution, from a Marxist standpoint it tends to extract more of the social surplus value of productive activities for its own ends (that is, for the personal ends of individual bureaucrats within the state) (p. 31).[34]

Under statist forms of socialism, the worker is oppressed by collective institutions that are essentially inaccessible and largely outside the sphere of critique. The worker lives in a brave new world of domination and subordination, dehumanized under an unending stream of unlimited political authority and violence. Thus Marković stresses:

to *humanize radically* the contemporary world means to create conditions in which each individual can participate in the control of the enormous social and technical forces which man has at his disposal. An essential condition of such fundamental human liberation is the *abolition of any concentration of political and economic power in the hands of any particular social group.*

The abolition (*Aufhebung*) of private ownership of the means of production and the abolition of capitalists as a class is the first decisive step in this direction. The abolition of politics as a profession which enables a social group permanently to control social operations, and the abolition of bureaucracy as privileged elite is the second decisive step. Each is a *necessary* condition of a radical humanization, but only both taken together constitute its *sufficient* condition. (1974: 81)[35]

But, as Hayek has shown, the attempt to overthrow the market must place power in the hands of a few planners. And yet they will lack the epistemological capability to rationally control and coordinate the system. Both conditions—abolishing economic power and abolishing political power—cannot be simultaneously enjoyed as the praxis ideal claims. Interfering with or outright destroying market exchange will only increase political power and leave in its wake economic chaos.

The Praxis group maintains that statism is not the necessary outcome of abolishing (at least to some degree) spontaneous market relations per se. Rather, they seem to consider totalitarian centralization to be an undesirable consequence of Marx's revolutionary strategy of the dictatorship of the proletariat—which it also is—but they have traditionally failed to offer an alternative that is consistent with the Marxist praxis project that they helped revive.[36]

DECENTRALIZED PLANNING UNDER SELF-MANAGEMENT?

The Praxis philosophers have called for what they consider a radical—and realizable—alternative to the statist model, namely, a decentralized socialist system of workers' self-management, a system which they believe comes closest to the spirit of Marx's humanistic vision. Although they point to workers' self-management as a possible solution to both market and state alienation, they have not developed a systematic economic theory of the system. What are the economic characteristics of this system? How would planning and coordination be established? Though it intends to solve problems of political and economic alienation, how would self-managed socialism solve the fundamental economic problem of rationally allocating scarce resources for the betterment of the human community? Unfortunately, the praxis philosophers have few answers, if any. Because they have a one-sided emphasis on praxis, the Yugoslav philosophers have traditionally remained weak on the economic issues of planning and coordination. Svetozar Stojanović's recent plea for paying greater attention to the possibility of the Marxian vision is truly an exercise in self-criticism.

Without coming to terms with the problem of conveying and using scarce knowledge in a complex economic system, their limited (though important) emphasis on the realization of the praxis side of Marxian socialism fails to systematically take into account the economic knowledge problem, a problem which ever grows behind the back of praxis philosophy.

We must look elsewhere for an economic model of workers' self-management under nonmarket socialism. Perhaps the best description that approaches this form was provided by G. D. H. Cole in his 1935 book, *Economic Planning* (Cole 1971: esp. 313-52). Trying to develop an organizational economic model of self-managed socialism, Cole unintentionally provides a shining example of the inherent tension between the ideal of decentralization and the necessity of centralization. For example, although Cole recognized the political danger of a central planning bureau, he nevertheless acknowledged its necessity (in principle) to coordinate the economic activities of self-managed work units. He called for a National Planning Authority that would

embrace within its functions the allocation of resources to the production of producers' goods, including capital goods, as well as consumers' goods. It will have the power to decide . . . what proportion of the available productive resources is to be set aside for the production of future wealth, and how these resources are to be distributed among the different industries and services. (p. 327)

Yet Cole offers nothing more than a hope that decentralization will offset the dangers that result from a concentration of state power:

Regional decentralization has the advantage not only of preventing congestion at the center and the growth of top-heavy units of organization too large and cumbersome to be effectively controlled, but also of spreading responsibility over a wider field. . . . The more decentralized the system is, within the limits set by the need for unified organization, the more safeguards are there that it will be democratically administered in fact as well as in theory. It is, however, essential to stress the point that at any rate in a relatively small country, and I think in all countries in the earlier stages of planning . . . the residual powers and ultimate controlling authority must remain unified in the hands of a central body, and must not be broken up among a number of separate regions. This is indispensable if the system is to work out aright. (p. 335)

Though "it will be essential, in the stage of the transition, to create from above the controlling authorities which are to carry through the change and organize the socialized industries as sections of the new planned economy" (p. 347), he tries to assure the reader that

the long run aspiration of a planned economy must be to make each industry to the fullest possible extent a democratic self-governing Guild, responsible in matters of public policy to society as a whole, but left free, in the execution of the policy prescribed to it by society, to manage its internal affairs mainly in its own way. (p. 350)

And although "the last word in revising plans must come from the centre," Cole maintains that "the centre need be no more than a co-ordinating and revising authority, working on the basis of spontaneous proposals coming up to it from every possible source" (p. 344). That is enough, however, to assure the breakdown in the autonomy of the self-managed enterprises.[37]

The few economic models that have proposed participatory, decentralized socialism without market exchange do not seem to provide a satisfactory answer to the knowledge and totalitarian problems that unintentionally develop when the market is replaced by a unified plan. They do not address, formulate, or realize the existence of, let alone answer, the problem of rational economic calculation, not even from the point of view of the alleged Lange "solution." Instead, these models continue to struggle with the tension that began with Marx. They have yet to offer a viable, non-utopian solution.[38]

SELF-MANAGED MARKET SOCIALISM: AN ANSWER TO THE TENSION?

"Here lies the main problem of the Marxist approach: the abolition of the market is, at the same time, the abolition of the economic base for equality and freedom," observes Radoslav Selucký (1979: 21). Selucký argues, in ways similar to Hayek, that "centralism [and thus inequality and tyranny] is an inevitable price which must be paid for the abolition of the market" (p. 34).[39]

Familiar with contemporary economics, Selucký argues that the market is a knowledge-enhancing institution. Meaningful self-management requires the market, because the market allows for true autonomy between enterprises and disseminates scarce knowledge. A decentralized and voluntarily coordinated economic base, as it were, is necessary for a decentralized and voluntarily coordinated political superstructure. Selucký argues that Marx failed to understand the relationship between economic and political freedom, and thus harbored a utopian interpretation of praxis and de-alienation.[40]

The economic system of decentralized socialism characterized by workers' self-management, limited market exchange, and social property relations has been developed in theoretical detail primarily by Yugoslav economists, such as Branko Horvat. The theoretical model advanced by Horvat and others is thought to provide a contemporary answer to the Mises-Hayek critique of calculation under socialism. In fact, the goal of Horvat's magnum opus, *The Political Economy of Socialism* (1982), is to challenge the Austrian position on planning:

Hayek framed his argument so as to prove the superiority of the free market over central planning. In the context of this book, it may be of some historical interest to note the following claim made by Hayek in 1945: "nobody has yet succeeded in designing an alternative system in which certain features of the existing one can be preserved which are dear even to those who most violently assail it—such as particularly the extent to which the individual can choose his pursuits and consequently freely use his own knowledge and skills".... I shall not leave this challenge unanswered. (p. 577, n. 56)

To be sure, Horvat believes he answers Hayek:

a labor-managed economy is likely to operate much closer to the textbook model of the competitive market. Social ownership *implies planning*, but *does not eliminate the market*. Consequently, the labor-managed economy achieves exactly what Hayek considered to be impossible: an alternative form of organization in which genuine autonomy on the part of the firm is rendered compatible with *ex ante* coordination of economic activities and full use is made of the existing knowledge while losses due to market failures are avoided. (p. 208)

Socialist economy implies a market and autonomous, self-managing productive units. Consequently, a socialist firm can do anything a capitalist firm can do productively. The socialist economy, based on social property, also implies social planning. It can thus achieve all the productive effects that a centrally planned economy can. Since it is at least as efficient as each of the alternatives, and capable of achieving something else besides, it is more efficient. (p. 209)

We have, consequently, moved full circle in this chapter. When Mill, Ely, and the other late classical economists discussed the potential of workers' cooperation, they did not intend to abolish the market. Instead, they saw cooperatives (and state intervention, to varying degrees) as means for improving the market system. Influenced by the socialist calculation debate, Selucký, Horvat, and other contemporary social scientists who advocate workers' self-managed socialism apparently differ from their praxis philosopher colleagues: They now argue that the market is a means to improve the worker-managed socialist system. They seem to believe that the market generates scarce information for rational economic calculation and acts as a middle-of-the-road institution that provides a way out of the struggle between decentralization on the one side and centralization on the other.

The economics profession has, accordingly, developed theories of the behavior of self-managed firms under abstract equilibrium conditions, while eschewing problems concerning socialist economic calculation (the knowledge problem) and tensions between centralization and decentralization in self-managed socialism (the totalitarian problem). The contemporary debate has thus shifted to the interesting, though more narrow and less fundamental, problem of the self-managed firm's ability to realize appropriate and efficient incentives with respect to output, employment, and investment decisions. I believe it has failed, however, to study the restricted nature of the market process in the blueprint of self-managed socialism (of Horvat, for instance), and simply tends to assume that self-managed firms behave under conditions of full and complete information (or their probabilistic counterparts). Therefore I shall critically assess the development of the economic theory of the self-managed firm in the next chapter.

NOTES

1. Preface to the third edition. But Mill wanted to make it clear that he disagreed with movements that, in the name of socialism, condemned market competition: "While I agree and sympathize with Socialists in this practical portion of their aims," remarked Mill, "I utterly dissent from the conspicuous and vehement part of their teaching, their declamations against competition." "Competition may not be the best conceivable stimulus," he maintained, "but it is at present a necessary one, and no one can foresee the time when it will not be indispensable to progress" (1926: 792-93).

2. Fawcett maintained in his *Manual of Political Economy* (1888) that "we may look with more confidence to cooperation than to any other economic agency to improve the industrial conditions of the country" (p. 280).

3. Marshall added a caveat, however. He fought against the idea of centralizing the cooperative movement, for it would, in the end, crush the more spontaneous elements he thought were necessary for cooperation to prosper.

4. In this respect Walker anticipated Frank Knight's entrepreneur theory of the firm. See Knight (1971: 264-312). For a fuller discussion of entrepreneurship see Kirzner (1973; 1979).

5. Walker also mentions that the skills of an entrepreneur are largely tacit: "A kind of subtle instinct often directs the movements of the ablest merchants, bankers, and manufacturers. . . . They not only could not give reasons intelligible to others for the course they take; they do not even analyze their intellectual processes for their own satisfaction" (1968: 251-52).

6. He did, however, see much to be gained through profit sharing and consumers' cooperation (1968: 282-88).

7. I shall discuss this group of cooperatives in chapter 6.

8. See the empirical studies by Derek Jones (1979; 1980; 1982).

9. Cf. Perlman (1949: 179): "The eighties . . . saw the beginning of a continuous contact between intellectuals and the labor movement, when Professor Richard T. Ely of Johns Hopkins University and his students applied themselves to a study of the labor movement." Elsewhere Perlman notes that Ely, interested in the Knights

of Labor (the labor union that proclaimed to take an active role in establishing producer cooperatives), had encouraged his students to join the Knights in order to better understand the labor movement (Perlman 1937: 72, n. 1).

10. Richard Hofstadter observes that "the social gospel was linked to academic economists who were beginning to criticize individualism" (1945: 88). Hofstadter notes that a close connection was formed between church administrators and the economics profession through the efforts of Ely, Commons, and others who established the American Economics Association. Although these economists wished to rid the social sciences of atomistic individualism, static theorizing, and a conservative rationalization of existing social institutions by placing more attention on history as opposed to theory (a promising methodological move), their account of the cooperative movement (especially Ely's) was unfortunately misleading. Perhaps because they were inclined to reject systematic theory altogether (a confused methodological move), they mistook their intellectual, progressive point of view for the point of view of the subjects they were studying (see Perlman 1949: 281). To put it simply, the intellectual's idea of freedom did not mesh with that of the laborers they were studying (Perlman 1949: 289-90).

11. See, in addition to the recent statistical work of Jones already cited, Beard (1969: 126), Catlin (1926: 572), Commons (1911: 136), Commons and Associates (1926: 430-38), Fetter (1922: 334), Millis and Montgomery (1945, vol. 3: 336-37), Perlman (1937: 128-29), and Virtue (1932).

12. For example, several cooperatives were formed during the nineteenth century in response to boss shop lockouts during labor disputes, with the goal to strengthen workers' bargaining power with the boss shops. Their dissolution need not reflect failure as such. In fact, it may represent the achievement of the workers' goals. As Rothschild and Whitt put it, this type of cooperative undertaking "was conceived as a temporary solution to a problem, and its disappearance meant, in effect, that the workers had been successful in their efforts" (1986: 78).

13. Ely merely concluded that, though still desirable, "Both profit sharing and cooperation have quite narrow limits at the present time" (1971: 482).

14. In his *Description of Industry* (1918), H. C. Adams called for the ideal of the "cooperative" system, but now Adams, like most others, understood cooperation to mean the whole panoply of industrial reforms that were proposed by the economics profession, rather than the development of consumers' and producers' cooperatives (cf. Dorfman 1969, vol. 5: 401-2). State regulation and planning, encouraged largely by corporate interests, became the hallmark of the Progressive Era in the United States. See Kolko (1963) and Weinstein (1968).

15. Merkle (1980) provides a good account of the development of scientific management.

16. The basic tenets of scientific management may be expressed as follows (Shafritz and Ott 1987: 21):

1. Organizations exist to accomplish production-related and economic goals.
2. There is one best way to organize for production, and that way can be found through systematic, scientific inquiry.
3. Production is maximized through specialization and division of labor.
4. People and organizations act in accordance with rational economic principles.

Once the best way to organize production is discovered, the role of the scientific manager is to impose the optimal procedure upon those working within the organization. There is little room for cooperation under such a system of workshop management.

17. The crux of these experiments lay in the time-and-motion studies of business operation. Here, meaningful human labor is reduced to a series of mechanical operations, operations which seek to increase output under the briefest time possible. Speed bosses, inspectors, time-study monitors and others collect and gather data into matrices of human physical motion, time, and output. The data is then formed into "rules, laws, and in many cases to mathematical formulae, which, with these new laws, are applied to the cooperation of the management to the work of the workmen" (1916: 72). In this way, and this way alone, the organization of the workshop is rendered "scientific."

18. See Shafritz and Ott (1987: 25) and Montgomery (1979: 26-27). Contrary to Taylor's goal, however, scientific management did not subvert unionism. Commons points out that labor unions were far from hostile to scientific management, because they were more interested in issues of distribution rather than production (Commons 1911). Unions were also willing to accept scientific management in return for closed shop recognition (Zerzan 1984).

19. See, for example, Henry Fayol's 1916 classic *General and Industrial Management* (Fayol 1949), where he claimed scientific management could be applied to bureaucratic governance structures.

20. Mitchell suggested that the scientific notions of central planning developed during the war would be used "for a long time to come, perhaps always" (quoted in Dorfman 1969, vol. 3: 490).

21. See Remington (1984: 113-45) for a detailed discussion of scientific rationalism in Bolshevik Russia, and in particular pp. 137-45 for the role of Taylorism.

22. The literature concerning the possibility of rational economic calculation under socialism is enormous. See Hayek (1945; 1975), Hoff (1949), Lange (1936), Lavoie (1981; 1985c; 1986a), Lerner (1934; 1944), Mises (1920; 1966: 698-715; 1981b), Murrel (1983), Schumpeter (1976: 172-99), Taylor (1929), Temkin (1989), and Vaughn (1980b). Lavoie's *Rivalry and Central Planning* (1985c) represents a major scholarly restatement and has greatly influenced my interpretation of the debate.

23. See Mises (1920: 112-16) and Lavoie (1985c: 67-74).

24. Mises further developed his argument in his 1922 treatise *Die Gemeinwirtschaft*. See Mises (1981b: 95-194). Both Max Weber (1978) and Boris Brutzkus (1935) had each independently arrived at conclusions similar to Mises (see Hayek 1975: 32-35).

25. In 1914 the Austrian economist and Fabian socialist Friedrich von Wieser drew a similar conclusion, without invoking the general equilibrium model. Wieser argued that coordination in a complex economy

will be executed far more effectively by thousands and millions of eyes, exerting as many wills; they will be balanced, one against the other, far more accurately than if all these actions, like some complex mechanism, had to be guided and directed by some superior control. A central prompter of this sort could never be informed of countless possibilities, to be met with in every individual case, as regards the utmost utility to be derived from given circumstances, or the best steps to be taken for future advancement and progress. (Wieser 1967: 396-97)

Also see Lavoie (1985c: 79-85).

26. Of course, this is true merely by assumption, for Lange assumes that consumer preferences, prices (in a "parametric," or perfectly competitive sense), and the amount of resources available are fully known to the central planners. In addition, he assumes given production functions. See Lange (1936: 60-61).

27. Cf. Lavoie: "If there is a satisfactory refutation of Lange, it must be one that is as critical of this 'auctioneer' equilibrating mechanism as it is of the central planning board, and for essentially the same reason. Neither auctioneer nor planning board could have the requisite knowledge" (1985c: 122).

28. And Lange did not seem aware of the fact that Barone himself expressed a profound reservation about the practical attempt to solve his theoretical model: "Many of the writers who have criticized collectivism," wrote Barone, "have hesitated to use as evidence the practical difficulties in establishing on paper the various equivalents; but it seems they have not perceived what really are the difficulties— or more frankly, the impossibility—of solving such equations a priori." Moreover, Barone concluded: "From what we have seen and demonstrated hitherto, it is obvious how fantastic those doctrines are which imagine that production in the collectivist regime would be ordered in a manner substantially different from that of 'anarchist' production" (Barone 1908: 287, 289).

29.

The static state can dispense with economic calculation. For here the events in economic life are ever recurring; and if we assume that the first disposition of the static socialist economy follows on the basis of the final state of the competitive economy, we might at all events conceive of a socialist production system which is rationally controlled from an economic point of view. But this is only conceptually possible. (Mises 1920: 109)

Also see his 1927 work, *Liberalismus* (translated as *Liberalism*), esp. his section devoted to "The Impracticability of Socialism" (Mises 1962: 70-75).

30. See, for example, the useful collection of classic and contemporary Austrian essays edited by Littlechild (1990). Also see the essays in Grassl and Smith (1986) for the historical roots of the Austrian school. Jaffe (1976) provides a nice discussion of the early years of marginalism and separates the spontaneous order theory of Carl Menger from the partial and general equilibrium theories of William Stanley Jevons and Leon Walras.

31. I do not believe Hayek conceded, but I do believe that both Hayek and Mises made a scholarly mistake by referring to the Soviet economic system as socialist, for, as I shall discuss momentarily, the Soviet system is not comprehensively planned, but rather, relies upon "polycentric" decision-making structures and market exchange. Mises and Hayek reserved the term "socialism" solely for the comprehensively planned organizational form. Undoubtedly, their irresponsible use of terms aggravated the confusion over just what they had meant during the calculation debate. Polanyi's criticism is valid:

Of all the intellectual triumphs of the Communist regime—and they are vast—it seems to me the greatest is to have made these eminent and influential writers so completely lose their heads. Could anything please that regime better than to hear itself proclaimed by its leading opponents as an omnipotent, omniscient, omnipresent socialist planner? That is precisely the picture of itself which the regime was so desperately struggling to keep up. Such accusations supply the Soviet government with an incontestable "testimony" of having achieved the impossible aspirations of socialism, when in fact it has simply set up a system of state capitalism—a goal which leaves the regime next door to where it started. (1957: 36)

32. Polanyi remarked: "in reality such an alleged plan is but a meaningless summary of an aggregate of plans, dressed up as a single plan" (1951: 134). Peter Rutland draws a complementary observation in his *The Myth of the Plan* (1985), where he demonstrates that planning in the Soviet system "is a very real *political* phenomenon, even if politics is about the erection and maintenance of public facades" (p. 260).

33. Cf. Andrija Krešić:

The concentration of the entire national economic potential in the hands of the state as the only real owner was certainly more rational from a purely economic point of view than the wastage of effort inherent in the fragmented and anarchic economy of private capitalism. . . . Through strictly centralized direction of the economy and through unified, centralized state management planning the already centralized state management developed and consolidated itself still further. Centralized planning tended to become absolute. (1968: 126-27)

34. But the growth of the state is still limited by economic constraints. Claus Offe argues that the state in capitalist society receives its revenue from the productive activities taking place within the market process. Because this relationship is parasitic, there is a limit on the amount of revenue it can extract from enterprises: extracting too much (in the form of taxes) may damage the market to such an extent that the parasite kills its host. Business people, accordingly, maintain a large degree of economic control and also enjoy some degree of political power. This view (although I do not know if Offe would agree) also supports the notion that the Soviet system is predominantly polycentric rather than a centrally planned economy, because it suggests that the Soviet state also confronts a limit on the extent to which it can intervene in market processes. In other words, the parasitic socialist state must continue to live off the productive activities of those it presumes to dominate, and it can only do so by allowing a critical degree of economic control at the level of individual enterprises. See Offe (1984). For a sympathetic critique of Offe's discussion of the welfare state, see Prychitko (1990d).

35. Marković's radicalism seems to verge on outright anarchism. But his collectivist stance reproduces the tension that we found in Marx. Although Marković envisions a decentralized, stateless order, his appeal to comprehensive planning through the *Aufhebung* of spontaneous market exchange allows the hierarchical structures of the state to return if the knowledge problem still persists. A fundamental coordination problem of "how to provide for the rationality of the whole process and at the same time the spontaneity of its individual parts" must be overcome (Marković 1975b: 479). Centralization seems unavoidable:

It is naive, to put it mildly, to think that rational guidance of overall social processes can be achieved by the spontaneous harmonization of individual local and regional plans, or by spontaneous vertical linking. Not only must one planning organization avoid negating the freedom of decision of others, but all organizations together, directly or indirectly, must set certain general frameworks to their freedom of planning, that is, to establish certain general objectives that should be achieved in a given time interval. Hence some democratically formed central institutions—in fact, central organs of self-government—are indispensable for the setting of such general objectives and the determination of the means and mechanisms for their fulfillment. (p. 486)

36. Svetozar Stojanović, for example, claims that the idea of the dictatorship of the proletariat was naive and utopian and Marx was therefore utterly irresponsible to promote it, because it could be used (and indeed was used) to support a spectrum of conflicting ideological missions (1988: 59-77). Marx, so careful to develop a "scientific socialism," failed terribly to clarify the meaning of the dictatorship of the proletariat—he advocated workers' self-management such as it arose under the Paris Commune, and yet considered only the communists to be the vanguard of the socialist revolution.

Stojanović argues that Marx the scientific socialist should have studied the actual possibilities (intended *and* unintended) of the dictatorship of the proletariat. Instead, however, he treated the idea as would any other utopian: he promised that the state would eventually wither away after the vanguard seized control of property. There is just as little empirical evidence to support Marx's claim that the state would eventually wither away under the dictatorship of the proletariat as there is to believe that Fourier's system would allow people to live for 144 years and drink from a sea of lemonade. But, because of his excessive anti-utopianism, Marx never bothered to systematically and realistically study the concrete problems of the transformation to full socialism.

"Certainly," Stojanović writes, "a theory that deliberately takes upon itself the responsibility for changing the world, must not in principle avoid the (co-)responsibility for its own fate in the world" (p. 62). Stojanović persuasively argues that the critic of ideology and alienation has a certain responsibility to ensure that his or her own ideas do not become another source of alienation and mere ideology. In a unique turn on Marx's Eleventh Thesis on Feuerbach—"Philosophers have only *interpreted* the world, in various ways; the point, however, is to *change* it"— Stojanović reinterprets it in light of contemporary statism:

In order to reduce the danger of the world being changed in an undesired direction, in the name of philosophy, and of philosophy itself being abused as an ideological justification for such change, the way of philosophizing about the world must be changed by focusing on the question of the realizability of that philosophy. (p. 76)

37. A recent attempt to model a marketless yet participatory, decentralized socialist system (Albert and Hahnel 1978) employs an abstract iterative checking procedure that is said to allow for planning to proceed from the "bottom up" rather than the "top down." The authors recognize that because "there is not reason to suppose that the initial proposals will provide an immediate mesh or economic plan," one can only conceive "the planning procedure as a potentially continuous process" (pp. 270, 271). But the procedure of proposing, rejecting, and counterproposing requires a hierarchy of (presumably democratic) bodies. That is, a vertical structure must be developed to smooth over the conflicts created by horizontal decision-making. And thus the devolution toward centralization: "Federations would be necessary. Every 'industry' would have regional councils with representatives from all the work-place councils, and national councils made up of representatives from all the regions" (p. 271).

Decision-making can be bumped up the hierarchy of councils only so long. If production and consumption are ever to start, someone (or some supreme council) must make a decision that binds all relevant parties. The supreme council must decide upon the best course of social action if chaos is not to be the rule. It must judge the merits of one plan over another. It must force inferior councils to accept a feasible plan. It will thus become, *de facto*, a central planning board. As Albert and Hahnel argue, "forcing mechanisms" will be required to establish plan convergence. What will guarantee that it will not become a vehicle of alienation? See Prychitko (1988: 132-39) for a more detailed criticism of the Albert-Hahnel model.

38. Cole later admitted that his socialist vision failed to accord with the behavior of concrete individuals:

Self-government—the conscious and continuous exercise of the art of citizenship—seemed to me not merely good in itself—which it is—but the good—which it is not. Accordingly, I constructed, along with other politically-minded persons a politically-minded person's Utopia of which, if it could ever exist, the ordinary man would certainly make hay by refusing to behave in the manner expected of him. (Cole quoted in Horvat 1982: 560, n. 24)

39. Selucký has been directly influenced by Friedman's discussion of the relationship between economic and political freedoms in his *Capitalism and Freedom* (Friedman 1962). See Selucký (1979: 135-41).

40. The "*definitive* resolution" of alienation is "unrealistic in political and utopian in economic terms" (Selucký 1979: 148-49). I should point out that the Praxis group's call for de-alienation does not necessarily imply, for some of them, that they believe self-managed socialism will put an absolute end to alienation. For example, Gajo Petrović writes:

Absolute de-alienation would be possible only if mankind were something given once and for all and unchangeable. Against advocates of absolute de-alienation, we may therefore maintain that only a relative de-alienation is possible. It is not possible to wipe out alienation because human "essence" or "nature" is not something given and unchangeable that could be fulfilled once and for all. But it is possible to create a basically non-alienated society that would stimulate the development of non-alienated, really human individuals. (1967: 151)

Consequently, as far as I see it, this brings a great degree of historicity into the notion of Marxism as revolutionary critique. If the praxis notion is historically relativized, it loses its ontological foundation, and must therefore be argued more in a pragmatic-persuasive fashion than on the grounds of an inevitable, absolutely certain future realization. It also opens the possibility for bringing the market back in, which has enormous consequences for revising Marx's system.

CHAPTER 4 _____

The Neoclassical Debate Over Incentives in the Self-Managed Enterprise

CHARACTERISTICS OF THE SELF-MANAGED ECONOMY

Between the anarchy of market systems and the totalitarianism of centrally planned systems is said to lay the workers' self-managed socialist system. It is considered a feasible alternative to either a fundamental market system and a centrally planned command economy in that it gives individuals the opportunity to participate in the workplace and in general social organization, while at the same time it allows the market to transmit scarce information in order to assist planning for an optimal allocation of resources. Accordingly, the tension between decentralization and centralization is considered solved (at the cost, however, of forsaking a good portion of the Marxist ideal). There is apparently little danger that the planning organs will devolve toward an increasingly hierarchical and centralized structure because the market is thought to adequately handle coordination and calculation problems by supplying all the necessary economic knowledge to allow for overall efficient decision-making.

Before I discuss the model of self-managed socialism, let us first consider the general model of a worker-managed market economy. Jaroslav Vanek outlines the general characteristics in his classic treatise *The General Theory of Labor-Managed Market Economies* (1970).[1]

First, the system is comprised of firms that are managed and controlled by the workers who compose each firm, on the democratic basis of one person, one vote. Workers are expected to participate directly in matters of general concern, and indirectly (through elected representatives) in other issues. Legal owners of assets invested in the firm do not have power of disposal of the firm's assets. Instead, economic control rests in the hands of those who actively participate in the management of the organization.

Second, all active participants share the "income" of the organization, defined as the difference between total revenue and total cost.[2] The distribution of income is egalitarian under a homogeneous labor force, and would equitably treat any differences that result from a heterogeneous labor force. Also, a collectively agreed upon portion of this income could be used for reserves, collective goods (such as housing and education), and investment in the firm itself.

Third, as a whole the workers' rights to the assets of the firm are *usufruct* rights, as opposed to the right of full economic ownership. In other words, the enterprise may rent real assets from the state, but cannot appropriate the full return from the loan or sale of these assets to other enterprises, nor destroy the value of its real assets. This is essentially a right whereby only those who actively participate in the enterprise may enjoy an income based on production itself, and not the purchase, sale, or destruction of real capital assets. The *usufruct* right is based entirely on each worker's active involvement in the enterprise, and is forfeited once the worker leaves the firm.

Fourth, the system is characterized by freedom of employment. Each individual worker is free to choose, refuse, or quit a job. Likewise, each enterprise reserves the right to hire or fire.

Finally, all buyers and sellers, whether households or enterprises, are assumed to exchange freely under perfectly competitive market prices. Only under cases of imperfect markets (brought about by externalities, public goods, or the presence of monopoly) is the state assumed to intervene in order to render the system more competitive.

Vanek points out that although these identifying characteristics have something in common with the only overall attempt to implement a self-managed system thus far—Yugoslavia—the model should not be thought of as a description of the Yugoslav economy, but a blueprint inspired by the attempt to implement self-management in Yugoslavia.[3]

SELF-MANAGEMENT AND SOCIAL PLANNING

Branko Horvat (1982) articulates many of the institutional details of the blueprint in order for it to accord more closely to the socialist aims of decentralization and workers' self-management.[4] For Horvat, a Marxist theory of socialism rests upon the notion of social ownership, which further implies workers' self-management and social planning.

Social ownership of the means of production is supposed to allow for an equal access to the means of production. Opposed to state management of capital goods, social ownership means workers' self-management. Horvat writes:

Socialism conceived as a self-governed society implies that there exists no particular class of owners of the means of production, either individual or collective. Everyone is equally an owner, which means that no one in particular is an owner. The specific feature of the Roman-bourgeois concept of property—the exclusion of others—is not applicable. If no one is excluded, then everyone has equal access to the means of production owned by society. As a consequence, property confers no special privileges. (1982: 236; cf. Vanek 1970: 315)

Social property, Horvat maintains, is the only property form consistent with Marxian exploitation theory because it negates the appropriation of income from property; hence, each productive member of society derives economic benefits solely from the act of work alone, and none from a mere claim to property. It therefore follows that social property implies the absence of command over others' labor power (1982: 237-39).

Horvat presumes that the overriding organizational goal within the self-managed firm is to maximize democracy in decision-making and to implement the decisions as efficiently as possible. Horvat argues that these organizational goals are not contradictory. Rather, they complement each other as long as the following criteria are met.

First, work groups within the organization must be able to engage in face-to-face communication. This means that work groups should be composed of relatively homogeneous members and must be small enough to achieve this objective. Horvat calls such a group a work unit, the basic economic unit in the self-managed system. The work unit is limited to a clearly defined and identified function that is not performed by other organizational groups within the enterprise. Work units are federated into a work community. In other words, as economic units, they federate to form the enterprise (pp. 240-41).

Second, decision-making within each work unit cannot be treated separately, in isolation. In many cases the decision of one work unit will substantially affect the concerns of other work units. This necessitates a second-level decision-making unit (the workers' council) that enjoys the right of decision-making in order to coordinate the activities of the individual work units it oversees. The workers' council is, by Horvat's design, a central legislative body delegated by the lower-order work units (p. 241).

To ensure correct and efficient decision-making, Horvat argues that the right of democratic decision-making must also entail responsibility for these decisions. Moreover, Horvat maintains, although the decision-making process should be as democratic as possible, *implementing* decisions "is a matter of professional competence, not of democracy" (p. 241). Consequently, Horvat's blueprint separates what he terms the "interest sphere" (value judgements and policy decisions) from the "professional sphere" (the technical implementation of the decisions arrived at in the interest sphere).[5]

The self-managed socialist enterprise is designed to overcome the split between capital and labor, and to break down the instrumental, hierarchical organizational form such as that advanced by the scientific management movement I discussed in the previous chapter. It also attempts to overcome the hierarchy imposed in the name of socialist democratic centralism, which, following Lenin, implies that administrators are appointed by the planning hierarchy, rather than being delegated by the workers themselves, and are solely accountable to their higher-level superiors, rather than to those whom they manage below (p. 188).

Along with self-management at the enterprise level, Horvat maintains that social ownership also implies social planning, as opposed to command planning. But, contrary to Marx and contemporary advocates of non-market self-managed socialism, Horvat does not want to abolish all market relations. He has been influenced by the socialist calculation debate earlier this century. Horvat acknowledges that "the market is a mechanism for communicating information," information which would become less useful if aggregated for central planning purposes: "Centralization," Horvat emphasizes, "implies substantial *loss and distortion of information*, which must be filtered through various layers of the hierarchy; in other words, it implies a tremendous waste of the knowledge available to society" (p. 200).[6] It is nevertheless a well-tempered rather than anarchic market, as Horvat insists in the following passage:

We wish to preserve essential consumer sovereignty because socialism is based on the preferences of the individuals who constitute the society. We also wish to preserve the autonomy of producers, since this is the precondition for self-management. When these are taken together, we need a market. But not a laissez-faire market. We need a market that will perform these two functions just stated, neither more nor less. In other words, we need *the market as a planning device* in a strictly defined sphere of priorities. In order to make it work properly, the . . . imperfections of the market should be corrected by planning interventions. This, in turn, means that we need *planning as a precondition for an efficient market*. (p. 332)

Information regarding consumer preferences will be generated by the market, and will be used to inform the plan; the plan will in turn rationalize production and consumption activities by designing conditions under which they appear perfectly competitive. Thus market and plan are considered complements. For Horvat,

Planning means the perfection of market choices in order to increase the economic welfare of the community. Far from being incompatible or contradictory, market and planning appear complementary, as two sides of the same coin. Neither is a goal in itself. Both are means for the appropriate organization of a socialist economy. (p. 332)[7]

THE FIRST SPARK OF THE DEBATE: WARD'S ILLYRIAN FIRM

The economic model of the workers' self-managed socialist economy is said to combine social property with planning and market exchange. This not only represents a turn from the orthodox Marxist vision of socialism; it also moves away from the contemporary praxis vision.[8]

One would think this model would be subject to critical debate from a comparative systems perspective. But, on the contrary, there has been remarkably little quarrel among economists that the economic organization of the worker-managed system is indeed socialist.[9] Svetozar Pejovich, one of the most persistent critics of the self-managed system, wrote that the Yugoslav-style system is "unique" in the way it "contains characteristics of both a centrally planned and a free-market economy," and concluded that "its emergence therefore represents a major innovation in the economics of socialism" (1966: ix-x).

Rather than a debate over markets, planning, and comparative economic organization, the main debate in the economics of workers' self-management has instead focused on the issue of incentives within the firm. Three decades ago in his article "The Firm in Illyria: Market Syndicalism," Benjamin Ward (1958) raised the question of whether a system characterized by workers' self-management of enterprises provides the appropriate economic incentives to assure an efficient allocation of scarce resources.

Ward wished to pick up where the great socialist calculation debate of the 1920s and 30s ended. Ward observed the reforms taking place in Eastern Europe at the time, especially in Yugoslavia, where the use of the market was becoming evident. "Market socialism" had become "something more than a theoretical counterexample." It was put in practice. "But as a serious proposal for reform," Ward maintained, "it leaves some important questions unanswered" (1958: 566). What are the important questions, and how does one go about answering them?

For Ward, the questions invariably center around the issue of equilibrium. Put simply, how does the output of the Illyrian firm[10] in perfectly competitive conditions compare to that of its capitalist counterpart?

Ward adopted the traditional neoclassical tools used to formally model the capitalist firm. He assumed that the objective function of the self-managed firm is to maximize net income per worker. In the self-managed firm, this dividend represents the difference between total revenue and the cost of capital and materials.[11] The Wardian single output, single variable input model may be defined as follows:

$$y = \frac{pq - R}{L}$$

where

p is the perfectly competitive price of the output,

q is the output associated with the short run production function such that $q = f(L,K)$ and K is fixed,

R is the fixed cost of capital,

L is the number of workers in the firm.

The short run equilibrium condition is obtained by differentiating the objective function with respect to L. The first order condition is derived as:

$$\frac{dy}{dL} = p\frac{dq}{dL}\left(\frac{1}{L}\right) - pq\left(\frac{1}{L^2}\right) + R\left(\frac{1}{L^2}\right) = 0$$

$$p\frac{dq}{dL} = pq\left(\frac{1}{L}\right) - R\left(\frac{1}{L}\right)$$

$$p\frac{dq}{dL} = y$$

Hence the economic behavior of the self-managed firm in the short run is similar to that of the traditional capitalist firm; namely, the self-managed firm will produce to the point where net income per laborer equals the marginal value product of labor.[12]

Consequently, using the standard tools for the economics of the self-managed firms brings forth some familiar neoclassical results. Ward, however, quickly demonstrated a strong counter-intuitive conclusion. Ward rearranged the first order condition in the following manner: since

$$p\frac{dq}{dL}\left(\frac{1}{L}\right) - pq\left(\frac{1}{L^2}\right) + R\left(\frac{1}{L^2}\right) = 0$$

then

$$q\left(\frac{1}{L}\right) - \frac{dq}{dL} = R\left(\frac{1}{pL}\right)$$

(That is, he expresses the left side of the equation in terms of the average product of labor and the marginal product of labor.)

How would the self-managed firm respond, asked Ward, to a change in the price of the product? An increase in p implies, under equilibrium, that the left side of the equation must decrease. Obviously, the difference between $q(1/L)$, the average product of labor, and dq/dL, the marginal product of labor, must become smaller, which, under diminishing marginal returns to labor, necessarily implies that the number of workers employed (and thus output) will decrease. Likewise, a decrease in p corresponds to an increase in the difference between the average product and marginal product of labor, which implies an increase in labor and output.[13]

Ward deduced the following alarming conclusion about the single output, single variable self-managed firm: In the short run, output responds inversely to changes in the product's price. Hence, the short run supply curve of the self-managed firm must be backward-bending, and therefore the threat of market instability is immanent. And the danger of instability is compounded, of course, in an economy which consists only of self-managed enterprises.

By casting his analysis in the metaphor of perfectly competitive system, Ward provided the foundation for the contemporary debate: it is argued primarily, if not exclusively, in formal, neoclassical language. The contemporary conversation reflects the questions Ward raised concerning the equilibrium conditions of the self-managed enterprise. These questions, in turn, are constrained by the method Ward chose to adopt.[14]

DOMAR'S CHARGE OF UNREALISM

Evsey Domar criticized Ward's model in his study of the Soviet kolkhoz (1966). Referring to it as the "Pure Model" (a term used to connote over-abstractness), Domar writes: Ward's " 'Pure Model,' for all its interesting and amusing (I hope) paradox, has one slight defect: it is unreal" (1966: 742).[15]

Domar was dissatisfied with Ward's assumptions. Specifically, Ward assumed labor input could be varied at will (hiring in the case of a fall in the price of the output or an increase in rent, and firing in the opposite case). But allowing for a nonchalant procedure to hire and fire members at will contradicts the basic nature or goal of a cooperative enterprise, which, Domar claims, is constant membership. By replacing Ward's assumption (that every worker is also a member of the enterprise) with one that allows constant membership and/or hiring additional wage laborers, then output is more likely to respond positively with increases in price and negatively with increases in rent.

Hired labor, however, does not seem to accord well with self-managed socialism. Consequently, Domar constructed an abstract equilibrium model (although he did not belittle it as a "pure model") of a self-managed enterprise with two products and two variable factors. With these new assumptions, Domar demonstrated that an increase in the price of one output will likely lead to increased production of that output, and a decreased production of the other output (whose relative price decreases—a basic substitution effect). Given that the self-managed enterprise maximizes net income per worker as opposed to profit, Domar demonstrated that the substitution effect will be offset somewhat by an income effect, and thereby concluded that the output supply curve is likely to be positively sloped, though it will nevertheless be less elastic than the capitalist counterpart. By altering the initial assumptions, Domar apparently put to rest the Wardian conclusion of market instability due to a backward bending supply curve.

LATER CRITICISMS OF WARD'S MODEL

Not entirely satisfied with Domar's criticism of Ward, Horvat further pursued the issue (1967; 1975b). Once again the charge of unrealism resounded, as Horvat attempted to construct a "more realistic" objective function.[16] Horvat asked if the "firm run by a workers' council really behave[s] in the assumed way" suggested by Ward (1975b: 231). Appealing to Occam's razor, he argued that economists should not model the objective function on the income-per-worker assumption and then simply riddle it with numerous special assumptions, even if, like Domar's, they are considered more realistic. Horvat postulated what he believed to be a much more realistic objective function—one which maximizes total profit rather than net income per worker. He defined profit as total revenue minus the cost of capital in addition to a level of personal income the workers aspire to achieve over the course of the accounting year (the aspired income performs the same role as the wage rate). Horvat then demonstrated that the equilibrium conditions for the self-managed firm will be identical to the capitalist counterpart, and, again, the Wardian instability implications disappear.

Since then, countless other parametric variations to the Ward model have appeared in the neoclassical literature. For example, Miyazaki and Neary (1983) analyze the effect the change in the price of the product has upon the demand for labor in terms of the Slutsky-style income and substitution effects. Meade (1972), Conte (1979; 1980), and Ben-Ner (1984) demonstrate a panoply of conclusions that may be drawn by simple changes in labor market assumptions. Bonin (1977), Ireland and Law (1978; 1981), Steinherr and Thisse (1979a), Brewer and Browning (1982) and a growing number of others continue to question Ward's initial conclusions. Nor do Ward's conclusions seem to hold in the long run. For example, James Meade (1979) has considered the long run equilibrium conditions of the basic model, and concludes that, as long as free entry and exit are allowed, in most cases the self-managed enterprise will perform just like its capitalist counterpart, and the fear of market instability disappears. The importance of long run entry is also stressed by Vanek (1970: 281-88), Sacks (1973), and Ichiishi (1977).

However, one cannot fail to see that the equilibrium outcomes are determined by the specification of the objective function and the assumptions embedded within. In short, the outcomes of the model reflect the assumptions of the model itself. This holds for the case of investment as well, to which I shall now turn.

FURUBOTN AND PEJOVICH: ATTENUATED PROPERTY RIGHTS AND THE INCENTIVE TO INVEST

The efficiency of the self-managed firm has also been questioned from the property rights approach of Svetozar Pejovich and Eirik Furubotn. The authors believe that they explicated an implicit property rights approach in the models of Ward and Domar (Furubotn and Pejovich 1972: 1156, n. 17; 1974b: 170, n. 1). Their adjustment to the basic model came about by introducing what they consider to be the "more relevant goal" of wealth into the objective function, as opposed to wages (Furubotn and Pejovich 1970: 434). Wealth maximization implies that workers attempt to maximize the present value of their expected future earnings, and thus allows for a multi-period model of the self-managed firm.

Furubotn and Pejovich assumed that the workers face two investment possibilities: They may invest in the enterprise itself, ploughing current wealth back in the form of capital goods, with the hope that the increased capital stock will fetch enhanced future wealth; or they may choose to invest current wealth outside the enterprise, in financial assets such as savings accounts, durable consumer goods, human capital, and so forth. Time preference among workers and each worker's expected tenure with the enterprise will thereby influence the choice between present and future consumption.

But that is not all. Given these assumptions, Furubotn and Pejovich added that the property rights assignments of the assets within the firm will necessarily determine the rate of investment within the firm.

If workers enjoy full property rights to the assets in the enterprise, each worker would optimally adjust investment to fit his or her time preference.[17] But the self-managed system is characterized by "attenuated" property rights: workers enjoy only a *usufruct* right to the assets in the enterprise, such that any individual worker enjoys an income based on his current participation in the enterprise. The worker has no claim to a portion of the future wealth of the enterprise upon exiting—he or she only owns a portion of the current residual. Furubotn and Pejovich concluded, a priori, that

this quasi-ownership must clearly be a shortened time horizon of the collective (which depends on the average length of employment expected by the majority of employees) and a high time preference rate relative to that which would prevail if the workers were granted the right of ownership over the assets acquired by the firm during the period of their employment. (1970: 443; cf. Pejovich 1973: 294-95)

Because workers enjoy full ownership of personal assets such as savings accounts and durable consumer goods, Furubotn and Pejovich argued that workers, being rational economic agents, will opt to invest the residual outside of the enterprise: the rate of return on owned assets will likely be much greater than the rate of return from investment in the non-owned capital stock of the self-managed enterprise.

Because the worker has no ownership claim to physical capital, and enjoys a share of the residual only by actively participating in the enterprise, the worker has a strong incentive to use his or her portion of the residual for saving and consumption rather than reinvesting it into the enterprise to encourage economic growth. Workers would reinvest the residual only if the expected rate of return on the business asset is very high or if their time preference is very low. To put it differently, financing the self-managed enterprise makes for a bad investment from the workers' point of view. They would rather save through an outside institution—one that offers a contracted rate of return plus recoverable principal.[18]

VANEK'S ASSUMPTION OF PERFECT CAPITAL MARKETS AND PLANNED INVESTMENT

Jaroslav Vanek agreed with the property rights economists that an extraordinarily high rate of return is necessary before workers will choose to internally finance the self-managed enterprise, and remarked that "The confusion and the inefficiency that this will generate in the allocation of scarce capital resources throughout the economy will be easily realized by anyone with even a rudimentary training in economics" (1977: 175). But this may not be as damning a *theoretical* criticism as the property rights economists claim, for Vanek maintained that the self-managed enterprises need not rely on self-financing, especially in the later stages of economic development. Again the claim of greater realism appears. As Vanek wrote:

If the assumption of no borrowing for the firm is replaced by a less stringent and more realistic one, permitting of partial external financing of projects—coupled possibly with future repayment from current income—the rate of return need no longer be far in excess of the market rate of interest (on private savings) to induce ploughing back of current income. (1970: 305)

In fact, Vanek went a step further (though by no means in the direction of greater realism) by assuming the existence of perfect capital markets, an assumption common to neoclassical economists in general and property rights economists in particular.[19] Under perfect capital markets, self-managed enterprises could borrow at a given rate of interest. Vanek postulated a supporting structure (the National Labor Management Agency) that performs the role of full external financing of self-managed firms (1970: ch. 15, esp. 315-20; also cf. Vanek 1971a). The National Labor Management Agency must also ensure that all other markets are perfectly competitive, so that it could "steer the economy to an optimal solution—that is, a solution with marginal rates of transformation and substitution equal" (1970: 374).

In short, the National Labor Management Agency must replace the conventional Walrasian auctioneer in order to bring about a Pareto-optimal general equilibrium. Assuming that it can do so (or at least do a better job than the capitalist economy, which in reality lacks a Walrasian-type coordinator), Vanek concluded:

Of key importance is the question whether the investment criteria of the labor-managed system produce an optimal allocation of capital resources in the economy. The answer is that provided that other markets operate perfectly, a perfect capital market will lead to a social optimum. If the condition of perfect competition in other markets—in particular the labor market (or quasi labor market)—is not fulfilled, then social optimum cannot be attained; but neither can it be obtained by a freely operating capitalist economy. (1970: 396)

Consequently, Vanek beat the property rights criticism on its own theoretical terms by assuming perfect capital markets to externally finance investment and encourage long term economic growth.

LIMITS TO THE NEOCLASSICAL APPROACH

"We are in possession," wrote Benjamin Ward, "of a correct analysis of the price system, . . . and an open-minded willingness to adapt our models to the burgeoning flow of empirical results" (1967: 509). (Over two decades later, however, one wonders to what extent the debate he inspired helps us really understand the nature of existing self-managed socialist systems, which was, recall, Ward's original goal.)

While our understanding of certain incentives problems (particularly the self-managed investment problem articulated by Furubotn, Pejovich, and Vanek) has increased, I dare say that our understanding of self-management from a knowledge transmission standpoint has increased little, if at all. To be sure, in addition to those already mentioned, numerous other reforms to the model have appeared by way of incorporating probabilistic uncertainty into the objective function;[20] respecifying the utility functions of the workers within the enterprise;[21] developing an implicit contracts approach;[22] applying game theory and studying the effects of coalitions;[23]

and analyzing the effects of imperfectly competitive market structures in the self-managed system.[24] And, without a doubt, Horvat's remark that Ward's original article "established a new discipline" should be taken literally (1986: 23). But the debate has focused primarily on the nature of the self-managed enterprise in the fictitious world of economic equilibrium and is steered in various directions with slight changes in the model's assumptions.

Horvat and other proponents of self-managed socialism defend that system from the standpoint of neoclassical economics. At first this may seem odd. The tools of neoclassical economics (indifference analysis, marginal value, the assumptions of perfect competition, and so forth) barely seem compatible with humanist socialist thought in general and (in Horvat's case) Marxian thought in particular. This combination, which goes back to Oskar Lange, appears contradictory to the history and spirit of socialist thought. But as G. B. Richardson (1959) once observed, the "capitalist" system depicted by the neoclassical model is ultimately not that of a laissez-faire, anarchic market, where prices emerge spontaneously through the rivalrous and cooperative efforts of buyers and sellers. Rather, the neoclassical framework models prices as given parameters that cannot be influenced by buyers or sellers. A single will coordinates all economic activities—the so-called Walrasian auctioneer. The standard competitive model is one in which the auctioneer fully determines the equilibrium prices and quantities for the entire array of commodities prior to barter-type exchange among isolated economic agents. Thus the basic neoclassical model, used to explain capitalist economic processes, may more accurately depict a centrally planned barter economy, as opposed to an anarchically organized monetary economy.[25]

Moreover, standard economists have become aware of the fact that the neoclassical model does not adequately describe real existing market phenomena. A fundamental shift of emphasis about the use of equilibrium has taken place since the 1950s and 1960s (see High 1990: ch. 1). Prior to that, Walras, Barone, Lange and some later economists such as Don Patinkin (1965: 38-39) argued that the market really solves the system of excess demand equations of general equilibrium theory (to varying degrees of efficiency).

More recently, however, leading neoclassical economists such as Kenneth Arrow and F. H. Hahn (1971) argue that the model is only about equilibrium as such. It is not about the actual operation of real world markets. From this viewpoint, which is becoming increasingly accepted today, it is a mistake to believe that the neoclassical theory describes markets or planning. It intends to do neither: it focuses only upon equilibrium states of affairs. The neoclassical model, as Hahn recently said, is

an abstract answer to an abstract and important question: Can a decentralized economy relying only on price signals for market information be orderly? The answer of General Equilibrium Theory is clear and definitive: One can describe such an economy with these properties. But this of course does not mean that any actual economy has been described. (1981: 126: cf. Hahn 1973)[26]

Early in the incentives problem debate, the participants seemed to believe that the equilibrium model describes capitalist markets and socialist self-management. With Arrow and Hahn, however, we find that the theory cannot do this adequately. Currently in the self-management literature, the model is used to discuss only the equilibrium properties of workers' self-management with apparently little regard for the real world dynamics. While this accords well with Arrow and Hahn, it does not (because it is not intended to) address a fundamental issue in comparative political economy, namely, the use of knowledge under alternative institutional settings. While the incentives problem debate has developed very clearly the equilibrium properties of self-managed enterprises (which is, admittedly, a tremendous intellectual feat), it has done so at the cost of overlooking some important questions in comparative systems.

Although the participants in the debate may differ on the efficiency of capitalist organization to self-managed organization, the participants as a whole have been guided by a common ground that goes deeper than the model itself. That common ground is the formalized notion of scientific truth. Both sides share a strong philosophical bias for a strictly formal model of economic explanation. Hence, what may appear as an instrumental debate, a debate in which each side merely chooses the assumptions that generate conclusions it seems motivated to defend, is really a manifestation of the problem of formalism as such. Although constrained by the language of neoclassical equilibrium theory, the debate over the incentives and efficiency of workers' self-management initially tried to be a debate over the realism and relevance of assumptions. Now it is a debate about equilibrium. It questions a parameter at a time. The implicit rules of the debate have not allowed the formal language as a whole to be challenged, for the formal model does not allow for critical self-reflection.[27]

TOWARD AN INTERPRETIVE TURN IN THE CONTEMPORARY DEBATE

The purpose of formalism is to remove personal judgement from the scientific realm (cf. Polanyi 1958: 119). In its call for greater exactitude and the elimination of ambiguity, formalist epistemology searches for an objective foundation from which to ground scientific knowledge. Without this foundation, the formalist argues, the question of just what constitutes valid knowledge and scientific truth cannot be answered. Hence, this thinking implies that *either* we have an objective foundation—a proven method, a set of rules—to secure knowledge, *or* our explanations of reality will be riddled with an all too human subjectivism, a subjectivism not open to rational examination.[28] Once the method is discovered (such as the procedure of equilibrium model building), explanation is reduced to questioning the model's various assumptions and predictions. The methodology—the commitment to formal modeling itself—is rarely, if ever, the subject of critical scrutiny.

The formal mode of explanation, however, does not allow for an explicit and committed attempt on behalf of the economist to understand the dialogical and truly spontaneous nature of the market process.

I am not arguing that all the participants in the debate over incentives in self-managed socialism are as abstract as Hahn and other general equilibrium theorists. Some seem to allow for interpretation at the edges of their studies. None are committed, however, to meaningful interpretation at the core of their theory. Moreover, the present direction which the research is taking is clearly toward increased formalization and abstraction—so much so that the earlier participants, such as Vanek, have lately expressed their reservations.

The positivist philosophy of science which the neoclassical paradigm is so deeply indebted to has fallen into disfavor in the contemporary philosophical discussion. Having abandoned the search for timeless, impersonal formulas to acquire scientific knowledge, contemporary philosophy of science has taken an "interpretive turn," to use Paul Rabinow and William Sullivan's phrase.[29]

The current understanding of the philosophy of science moves well beyond the prescriptions of formalism and positivism. Science is now seen as a spontaneously organized institution, an arena in which truth claims compete with one another, rather than a method or a set of criteria purported to advance truth. As Donald Polkinghorne rightly observes, contemporary philosophy of science differs from the past in that it "is not a school of thought"; rather "it is an attitude about knowledge" (1983: 279).[30]

The economic theory of workers' self-management needs to acquire this new attitude. Rather than divorcing itself from the meaningful interactions of the people within the system, it must come to terms with the human purposes and plans that are at the center of the social stage.

I believe that the major reason why the calculation argument advanced by Mises and Hayek in the 1920s and 30s had been theoretically misinterpreted by Lange, Lerner, and other participants as predominantly a motivation problem (finding ways to ensure that individuals would respond optimally to a set of given prices) is because the model of mainstream neoclassical economics was already formalized to such an extent that it could not adequately deal with complex social interaction (cf. Lavoie 1985c; 1986a). For instance, they failed to see that market signals are rooted in the intersubjectively shared meanings of the members of an economic community. Not only did Lange and his followers confuse the nature of the Mises-Hayek argument. I also believe that the participants in the contemporary debate over efficient incentives under self-managed socialism have fundamentally misunderstood the Austrian position as well.

The debate leaves much to be desired from the viewpoint of rational economic calculation under socialism. It has been restricted to an analysis of the nature of the self-managed firm—which is to say, it has largely been a debate in industrial organization instead of comparative political economy. Little, if any, attention has been given to workers' self-management as a dynamic economic system. Has the criticism of Mises and Hayek been answered by the advocates of self-managed socialism? The formalized language of the neoclassical model, from Ward's basic model to the most contemporary variants, unfortunately has not allowed a discussion of the use and transmission of inarticulate knowledge and unending processes of endogenous change, notions at the core of the Austrian criticism. The emphasis on incentives and equilibrium conditions, though useful for some questions, has completely displaced the question of how the socialist economy will generate knowledge in a form that allows for the discovery and rational allocation of scarce economic goods. Pointing to an exogenously given equilibrium price, optimal transfer prices, or perfect capital markets begs many fundamental questions.

Although Horvat nods to Mises and Hayek by allowing for some market exchange in order to ensure consumer sovereignty and producer autonomy, he nevertheless misunderstands the epistemological basis of the Austrian critique. In the next chapter, I shall demonstrate that the theory and practice of self-managed, Yugoslav-style socialism suffers from the knowledge problem and tensions between centralization and decentralization.

NOTES

1. These characteristics are also expanded upon in Vanek (1971b: ch. 2). Undoubtedly many blueprints of the worker-managed system abound in the economics of self-managed socialism. The key characteristics that Vanek mentions are, however, generally accepted throughout the literature, and therefore for my purpose there is no compelling reason to compare the intricacies between Vanek and the others. I shall, however, describe the institutional characteristics of self-managed socialism as provided by Horvat's (1982) comprehensive account, for it intends to be a Marxian variant of self-management and is closer to socialism in Yugoslavia.

2. This is labeled "income" rather than "profit" because profit is usually understood to include labor expense as a component of total cost; in the self-managed firm there is no objective cost of labor.

3. Vanek's model is intended to describe the universal characteristics of workers' self-management, and is not meant to necessarily describe a socialist system:

The labor-managed system need not even be socialist: the productive assets whose usufruct the workers enjoy might be procured or leased by banks or savings associations. Of course, there will be a great advantage if such functions are assumed by the society as a whole, represented by democratic government. Similarly, the labor-managed system need not even involve economic planning. The fact that it will function even if left entirely alone is one of its greatest strengths—although, . . . forecasting and some kind of indicative planning is highly desirable because it enhances considerably the efficiency of the system. Actually, the gains attributable to planning are far more significant in a labor-managed economy than in a capitalist economy; but the fact remains that planning should not be introduced as one of the definitions in the system. (1970: 7)

4. Horvat establishes what he explicitly considers a Marxist social theory as opposed to a general theory such as Vanek's, and hence emphasizes the necessity of *ex ante* planning as a fundamental element of worker-managed socialism.

5. "Policy decisions," Horvat writes, "are legitimized by political authority; executive and administrative work, by professional authority." Consequently, "in the interest sphere, the rule of one man, one vote applies; in the professional sphere, vote is weighed by professional competence" (p. 241).

Horvat is aware of the simplicity of his blueprint. He realizes, for instance, that work units will never be perfectly homogeneous nor sufficiently small; nor can the two spheres—the interest sphere and the professional sphere—be separated clearly. Hence control and conflict-solving institutions must be adopted in order to ensure that individuals or groups of individuals will not abuse power. Informed by an empirical study by Veljko Rus et al. (1977), Horvat points out that the greater the dispersion of power, the greater the conflicts that arise between individual groups:

Generally, the more equal the distribution of power, the greater is the uncertainty and the more conflict-ridden is the organization. The uncertainty caused by democratization may have integrative or disintegrative effects. In the former case, more numerous conflicts contribute to greater flexibility, greater responsiveness, and quicker crystallization of conflicts, which leads to improved efficiency. In the latter case, both interpersonal relations and efficiency may be disastrously affected. The self-management organization is thus very conflict sensitive. Consequently, an appropriate organization design and methods for conflict resolution appear extremely important for efficient decision making. (Horvat 1982: 259)

Unfortunately, Horvat does not provide a detailed model of conflict resolution. The danger of overwhelming conflicts of interest may cast into doubt the feasibility of Horvat's blueprint for the worker-managed firm. Moreover, Horvat's call for a split between the interest sphere and the professional sphere may bifurcate people's lives into civil and technical domains, and thus seems to move farther from the call of Marx.

6. Radoslav Selucký fully articulates the necessity for the market in the self-managed socialist system, an explanation which, like Horvat's, is also influenced by the calculation debate. He writes:

Although it would be foolish not to agree with Marx's suggestion that the market, as an *exclusive* regulator of economic processes, fails to maintain equilibrium and stimulate steady economic growth, it has been shown that, if the market is wholly eliminated and replaced in all its functions by the central plan, there is scarcely a *practical* possibility of rational economic calculation. Consequently, the mere abolition of the market is not a sufficient precondition for a more efficient functioning of socialist economic systems as compared with capitalist ones. That is why the traditional Marxian concept of direct allocation and distribution as the *exclusive* and *obligatory* socialist alternative to the market cannot be accepted. The plan may and should be used as a political tool for promoting preferential social values, for interfering with the objectiveless, spontaneous and impersonal market mechanism, for controlling, reg-

ulating, and taming it, for shaping the market according to societal priorities and for eliminating it from non-economic sectors, but never for replacing the market as *the* economic self-
regulator. While the plan could and should be powerful and superior to the market, it should
not become omnipotent; while it should serve as the means to an end, it should not become
an end in itself. (1979: 48)

7. Tom Bottomore claims that Horvat has thus "clearly formulated" the theoretical relationship between market and plan (1990: 89-90). While, in the realm
of abstract theory, market and plan may, perhaps, be considered complementary
(particularly in a Lange-type framework), it is nevertheless not at all clear how an
actual, dynamic market process as an *ex post* coordinator can be reconciled with
ex ante socialist planning.

8. The question of the transition period may arise here. Though the praxis
philosophers seem to allow for markets during the transition period, at least Mihailo
Marković clearly advocates the abolition of the market and commodity production
for the fully evolved socialist system. Marković stresses that "under conditions of
commodity production, self-management does not yet have *universal* human character. . . . To be sure, under the conditions of abundance, production for human
needs will gradually tend to replace production for profit" (1974: 237; also see
Marković 1964: 436; 1975a: 332; cf. Vranicki 1965). Horvat, on the contrary,
considers the transition period toward "socialism" to be that which leads to the
blueprint I have just described (see Horvat 1980; 1982: 415-94), and thus gives one
the impression that his "market-planned" blueprint is a post-transition model of
socialism.

9. There are exceptions, however. See, for example, Sweezy (1964). Certainly
Marx considered the elimination of the commodity mode of production and exchange to be a necessary (though not sufficient) condition for a system to be
socialist.

10. Ward uses the label "Illyrian" rather than Yugoslavian to denote a theoretical
idealization of the Yugoslav firm.

11. Ward includes a fixed wage as a cost of production (so that each worker
receives a wage payment in addition to his share of the net income). Because it
does not affect the short run conclusion that Ward draws in his model, for the sake
of simplicity I shall not include the fixed wage as an argument in the objective
function.

12. Similarly, in the event of fixed labor and variable capital, maximizing net
income per worker becomes the same as maximizing profit, where

$$y = \frac{pq - cK}{L}$$

and c is the price of capital.
Differentiating with respect to K, we derive the first order condition:

$$\frac{dy}{dK} = p\frac{dq}{dK}\left(\frac{1}{L}\right) - c\left(\frac{1}{L}\right) = 0$$

$$p\frac{dq}{dK} = c$$

Hence, the marginal value product of capital is equal to the price of capital.

13. Similarly, Ward shows that the self-managed firm will respond positively to a change in rent, or R (the cost of capital).

14. Ward's analysis is considered the first "modern" attempt to study the economics of workers' self-management (cf. Bonin and Putterman 1987: 3-4; Domar 1966: 734-5). The "modern" treatment differs from that of John Stuart Mill, F. A. Walker, and the others I discussed in the previous chapter because the modern analysis is thought to be more than a series of "comments." Rather, it is discussed in the language of a formal, equilibrium framework. Because the idea of being modern—and thus relevant—is directly linked with the ability to formally model economic phenomena, the analysis of the earlier economists on the subject of the self-managed firm is relegated to the history of economic thought and plays little part in the current discussion.

15. Domar, moreover, did not care for the policy implications of Ward's model, which he expressed in the following way:

Now a difficult (for an economic theorist) choice must be made between being original, if unrealistic, and being conventional and practical. For what could be more original and striking than recommendations derived from the "Pure Model," namely that rent should be increased (or imposed) and terms of trade turned against the peasants in order to make them work longer and harder for the kolkhoz? This would vindicate Stalin's agricultural policies, even though he had arrived at them without building models. (pp. 748-49)

16. For a good account of Horvat's 1967 argument, see Milenkovitch (1971: 204-10). Also see Vanek's criticism (1977: ch. 5).

17. Furubotn says that the attenuated property rights arrangement in the self-managed economy would "warp" an otherwise optimal scheme of investment incentives: "Obviously, if workers were permitted to own capital, each individual would be free to adjust investment optimally to his pattern of time preference" (1971: 197, n. 32).

18. Furubotn argues that, because the original group of workers in a self-managed enterprise have financed the capital of the enterprise, under diminishing returns to scale the original workers will have an incentive to limit employment in order not to dampen the average residual (the new workers, though making no financial sacrifice, nevertheless enjoy the same claim to the residual as the incumbent workers) (1971: 194-95). For a response, see Bonin's (1984) discussion of a balanced budget fiscal policy which, following a Ward-type model, is designed to increase membership of the self-managed enterprise through a discretionary use of a lump-sum tax.

19. See, for example, Manne (1965), Fama (1970), Jensen and Meckling (1979), and Jensen and Ruback (1983).

20. See, for example, Taub (1974), Dreze (1976), Bonin (1977; 1980), Muzondo (1979; 1980), Steinherr and Thisse (1979b), Inselbaq and Sertel (1979), and Hay and Suckling (1980).

21. See, for example, Sen (1966), Bonin (1977), Ben-Ner and Neuberger (1979), Israelsen (1980), Putterman (1980), and Ireland and Law (1981).

22. See Miyazaki and Neary (1983), Bonin (1984). Along with Bradley and Gelb (1981) and Putterman (1984), this recent literature is largely a response to the monitoring or principal-agent problems developed in the work of Alchian and

Demsetz (1972), Mirrlees (1976), Shavell (1979), Holmstrom (1979; 1982), and Malcomson (1984).

23. As provided by Ichiishi (1977), Staatz (1983), and Sexton (1986).

24. See Vanek (1970; 1971a), Meade (1974), Maurice and Ferguson (1976), Gal-Or, Landsberger, and Subotnik (1980), Landsberger and Subotnik (1980), Ireland and Law (1982), Hill and Waterson (1983), Neary (1984), and Estrin (1985). Two exhaustive surveys of the neoclassical economics of self-management are provided by Pryor (1983) and Bonin and Putterman (1987).

25. Thus an irony appears: advocates of decentralized socialism have embraced the standard neoclassical model, a model generally considered to illustrate the hypothetical capitalist economy; yet, if Richardson is correct, the standard model may be an equally if not more appropriate model for a hypothetical, centrally planned system. Now this irony, or what appears to be an irony, may be partly explained in terms of strategic pursuit. If one aims to convince other economists of the efficiency of a socialist regime, for example, then perhaps the best way to succeed is to adopt as much of the standard language as necessary—to play on the same turf—in order to be accepted. This strategy may appear fruitful during the initial stages of a debate between supporters of very different economic visions. All too often, however, adopting the other's language, although it is thought to allow meaningful conversation, unintentionally obstructs conversation. This occurred during the course of the socialist calculation debate (as I discussed in chapter 3) and it continues in the contemporary incentives debate.

26. Although Hahn speaks of general equilibrium theory, the argument applies to partial equilibrium theory as well. Fink (1991: ch. 1) demonstrates that partial equilibrium theory, if used consistently, must collapse into general equilibrium theory. Also see Cowen and Fink (1985).

27. Some economists are beginning to question the fruitfulness of this debate, which is well into its third decade. For example, after his excellent, sympathetic, and exhaustive review of the literature of producers' cooperatives and self-managed firms, Frederic L. Pryor candidly concludes:

If most existing models generate few testable propositions and if, further, there is little certainty that their assumptions apply to production cooperatives, what good are they? Have we not reached the point of diminishing returns with a proliferation of models with slightly different theoretical fillips and slightly different assumptions? In short, is most of the theoretical literature anything more than an academic game where the authors appear to have little knowledge of how such organizations actually work and, instead, wish to demonstrate their mathematical virtuosity?

In short, theoretical analyses have given us too many conflicting theories of behavior of production cooperatives. If we are to be able to say anything definite about such organizations, it is imperative to leave our armchairs and empirically to investigate how these cooperatives actually work. (1983: 163, 164)

To offset the misplaced emphasis of much of the literature and in the hope to improve our understanding of the self-managed system, Jaroslav Vanek has recently proposed that we critically assess the formal model in its totality. As he puts it:

The first important word is simplicity, and the first point I would like to make bears on the simplicity of theoretical analysis. With the increasing army of unemployed and underemployed establishment economists in the west, the notion of scientific progress has been entirely deformed and bastardized into the notion of increasing complexity with no regard to relevance. To begin with, the neo-classical tools of perfect markets, utility functions and production functions are sterile and incorrect. And if one starts building from these shaky building blocks high edifices, the results are even worse. These tools must be abandoned, and we must meticulously keep verifying the correctness and realism of our tools while keeping them simple so that the majority can use and understand them. . . .

What holds for economic theory also holds for empirical investigation. (1988: 2-3)

Until now only the "realism" of the assumptions have been subject to criticism, a criticism that yields increasingly abstract analyses whose relevance to the key questions of comparative political economy is slipping. Vanek's plea for moving well beyond the strictly neoclassical model is thus long overdue.

28. Richard Bernstein calls this struggle the "Cartesian Anxiety," whose roots trace back to Descartes's *Meditations*. See Bernstein (1983: 16-20).

29. According to Rabinow and Sullivan:

The interpretive turn refocuses attention on the concrete varieties of cultural meaning, in their particularity and complex texture, but without falling into traps of historicism or cultural relativism in their classical forms. For the human sciences both the object of investigation— the web of language, symbol, and institutions that constitutes signification—and the tools by which investigation is carried out share inescapably the same pervasive context that is the human world. . . . [T]he interpretive approach denies and, overcomes the almost de rigueur opposition of subjectivity and objectivity. . . . [I]nterpretation begins from the postulate that the web of meaning constitutes human existence to such an extent that it cannot ever be meaningfully reduced to constitutionally prior speech acts, dyadic relations, or predefined elements. Intentionality and empathy are rather seen as dependent on the prior existence of the shared world of meaning within which the subjects of human discourse constitute themselves. It is in this literal sense that interpretive social science can be called a return to the objective world, seeing the world as in the first instance the circle of meaning within which we find ourselves and which we can never fully surpass. (1979: 4-5)

30. A useful and growing body of literature concerning the interpretive philosophy of science is provided by Bernstein (1983), Gadamer (1985), Hekman (1986), Kuhn (1970), Polanyi (1958; 1959), Polkinghorne (1983), and Ricoeur (1976). The anthologies of Dallmayr and McCarthy (1977), Haan et al. (1983), Hollinger (1985), Mueller-Vollmer (1985), Natanson (1973), Rabinow and Sullivan (1979), and Truzzi (1974) are helpful introductions to the literature. For the interpretive approach to economics, see Boettke (1990a), Ebeling (1986, 1987), Lavoie (1985b; 1986b; 1991; forthcoming), and Madison (1989).

CHAPTER 5 _____

Self-Management and the Knowledge Problem: Tensions in the Theory and Practice of Yugoslav Socialism

Branko Horvat claims that social property implies both workers' self-management and *ex ante* social planning. While much of the neoclassical debate has focused on the equilibrium behavior of self-managed firms and incentives problems, little attention has been paid to knowledge problems inherent in social planning. As I pointed out in the previous chapter, the equilibrium framework allows for a discussion of motivation and incentives issues, but this comes at the cost of overlooking the type of knowledge transmitted in the market process and the way that knowledge can be employed in economic planning. I believe that Horvat's theory of self-managed socialism fails to come to terms with the knowledge problem. Horvat's theory, and Yugoslav reality, demonstrates the struggle between centralization and decentralization that has its roots in Marx.[1]

A MARKET-PLANNED SYSTEM?

Like Karl Marx, Horvat understands that the essence of economic planning is to achieve rational, *ex ante* coordination:

In order to make rational use of social productive capital and in order to reduce uncertainty enough so that self-management decisions produce the expected consequences, the activities of productive units must be coordinated on an *ex ante* basis, which is the essence of planning. . . . Without social planning, they would become victims of haphazard forces of an uncontrolled market. (1982: 230)

Social planning means participatory planning among all the self-managed enterprises, whose purpose is to create a coherent, coordinated system: "plans are formulated at all levels and then are gradually integrated into an overall plan by an iterative process of consultation and negotiation" (p. 333).[2]

Moreover, Horvat sincerely wishes to keep the system decentralized— to leave "each *individual* firm full autonomy—and responsibility—for decision-making" (p. 230). Self-managed socialism, *contra* Stalinism, requires a meaningful degree of autonomy among the associated producers. It also demands that citizens, as consumers, are free to pursue their preferences, rather than being sacrificed on behalf of the preferences of the Communist Party (as in the "buffer sector" of Soviet-style socialism).

Unlike Marx, however, Horvat maintains (as I mentioned in the previous chapter) that market exchange is necessary to ensure the autonomy of the socialist enterprises and to preserve consumer sovereignty. A market that performs these two functions, "neither less nor more," (p. 332) helps ensure that the Hayekian knowledge problem will be overcome and hence the tendency for totalitarian centralization will be reduced.

Yet Horvat's "neither less nor more" is the source of tremendous tension. How can a social economic plan, worthy of its name, be rationally advanced in a system with innumerable ("polycentric") planning centers? Too great a reliance upon the spontaneous institution of the market places control firmly in the hands of the worker-managed enterprise, and participation by other members in society would be drastically curtailed. It would shift the self-managed enterprise into a capitalistic context and thereby render the notion of social ownership a mere legal fiction and social planning an economic myth—something that Horvat cannot allow. That would collapse to a system of workers' cooperatives competing in an anarchic market process.[3]

Indeed, Horvat considers Yugoslavia during the 1960s to have gone much too far in the direction of the market (particularly after the 1965 economic reform). Yugoslavia moved from a self-described centrally planned system (1946-1950) toward a greater allowance and legitimation of market exchange. The call for central planning was replaced by a call for self-management and enhanced enterprise autonomy. Reforms in 1961 opened the Yugoslav economy to world markets and the international division of labor, partly decentralized the financial system, and gave workers a greater degree of control over wage determination.[4] Whereas investment decisions had been done completely on the basis of a centralized state plan (the Federal Investment Fund), by 1965 it was abandoned. The scope of state involvement in investment decisions was reduced, as workers within self-managed enterprises were allowed the autonomy to make investment decisions with their respective residuals. Although this phase of "market" socialism would thus seem to accord with Horvat's concern for consumer sovereignty and enterprise autonomy, it does not, however, fit with his notion of *ex ante* coordination through social planning.[5]

Horvat protests that "the reform was based on the naive idea that 'the working collectives know best what is good for them' " (a rather striking statement from a Marxist proponent of self-management). He continues:

That implied the dismantling of government investment funds and specialized federal banks; the reform resulted in the removal of most levers of effective planning and exclusive reliance on monetary policy (at first extremely restrictive). Generally the reform meant a revival of the nineteenth-century laissez-faire economic approach. No wonder that the economy immediately plunged into recession, and that within two years the rate of growth of industrial output fell below zero. (p. 206)[6]

He insists that

The socialist economy uses the market because this is the most efficient means available for achieving the targets of producers' and consumers' equality. But it is neither a laissez-faire nor a universal market. It is strictly regulated by social planning. And it is supplemented by an important segment of nonmarket activities whose importance grows with economic development. (p. 231)

Horvat struggles between market and plan. On the one hand he calls for a market to ensure autonomy on behalf of producers and consumers. On the other he tries to uphold the Marxian ideal of social planning. And yet he claims his theory of self-managed socialism is not grounded in a combination of market and plan, as in the notion of a "mixed economy."[7] How can we make sense of this?

Perhaps in the following way.

A spontaneous market process in the means of production contradicts a fundamental feature of social property: the need for planned, *ex ante* coordination. The market can only oppose the plan, for market activities as a whole are coordinated *ex post* through a ceaseless flux in relative price signals. The model of self-managed socialism cannot allow for "anarchic" enterprise autonomy, for the means of production are supposed to be socially owned and must be coordinated in a rational, planned manner. This logically requires centralization. Horvat argues at once that while "the system as a whole behaves as a polycentric system," nevertheless "The task of the federation is to integrate the functioning of all subsystems and thus ensure the overall functioning of the entire system" (p. 356). Indeed, when he speaks of planning, Horvat maintains that economic coordination can be achieved "only by centralized decision making for the country as a whole" (p. 362), and, at another point (buried in a footnote) he admits that "all planning is at least partly or in the final analysis central" (p. 586, n. 51).

In Horvat's theory of self-managed socialism, the role of spontaneously formed market prices seems limited to the allocation of consumer goods alone. Spontaneous pricing of capital goods is eliminated through the social planning requirement of self-managed socialism: "the task of the Planning Bureau is to accomplish *ex ante* coordination of economic activities on the basis of the relevant set of preferences" (p. 349). The notion of consumers' sovereignty—a market for consumer goods—will apparently supply the information that reveals "the relevant set of preferences."[8]

With this in mind, Horvat's argument that the market can be used to "inform" the plan becomes more understandable, in theory. The data supplied by the consumer goods market can be used to socially plan the capital structure, imputing the equilibrium values of lower-order goods to higher-order goods (the socially owned means of production). This is similar to Joseph Schumpeter's (1976: 175) claim (in defense of Oskar Lange's model) that equilibrium prices in the consumer goods market can be used to technically impute the values of corresponding higher-order capital goods. In fact, Horvat claims that

Though autonomous to a great extent, the kolektiv clearly cannot be completely autonomous. In matters of valuations which affect significantly the interests of some other kolektivs there must be a superior representative body to make decisions. . . . In matters with which we are primarily concerned the upwards dependence of kolektivs will be largely technical in nature. It would be ideal to separate "regulative" functions from "operative" functions and leave the former to the representative bodies while the latter should be displayed by the working kolektivs and their associations. In this way supreme co-ordination, including the Social Plan together with the financial instruments necessary to ensure its execution, would be vested in Parliament. It should be stressed, however, that a certain amount of co-ordination will have to be done by the specialized state apparatus on the spot, in which case regulative functions shade into operative ones. . . . Finally, the Planning Authority supplies enterprises with relevant data which provide elements for their economic policies. The enterprises report their own important decisions which enables the Planning Authority to prepare a new set of data for the use of all concerned. The Social Plan, the banks and the availability of information represent an efficient co-ordinating mechanism which enables smooth functioning of the economy without centralized management. The upshot of all of this is that risks and uncertainties are minimized and the entrepreneurial function presents itself in a completely new light. (1964: 299-300)

Horvat differs, fundamentally, from earlier market socialists in his call for social (rather than state) ownership and hence participatory, self-managed decision-making at all levels in society. But his argument that the coordination of production processes among the self-managed enterprises ("the upwards dependence of kolektivs") is predominantly a technical problem parallels the basic argument of Lange and Schumpeter.

THE KNOWLEDGE PROBLEM IN SELF-MANAGED SOCIALISM

The choice of the methods of production is not, however, a technical activity. It depends instead upon the tacit skills of entrepreneurial judgement and alertness to profit opportunities in a competitive market process. Now it may be possible that value could be theoretically imputed to higher order goods from equilibrium prices of consumer goods if each factor of production is perfectly substitutable or if each and every factor is absolutely specific. Then indeed, the problem to be solved would be fit for engineers. But in real existing dynamic systems, capital resources are inescapably heterogeneous.[9]

A tangible capital good can have many uses; perhaps, with advanced technology, even an infinite number of conflicting uses. Nevertheless, when a hierarchical or cooperative enterprise embarks upon production it must use capital in a certain, concrete way to form a unique plan. Without spontaneous market prices of capital goods to assist in calculating their economic value, even the relatively straightforward problem of which methods to choose and resources to use in the production of a single higher-order good will become an infinitely complex one.

In a society with advanced technology, a particular resource can be used to produce a multitude of goods. Consider all the different uses to which wood, plastic, and steel, for example, are currently used under the market system. How will a workers' council or system of councils evaluate the many, inevitably conflicting uses of a single resource? Upon what basis will it be decided that, for example, a railroad line will be constructed of steel as opposed to some other metal; or that the engine should be run on coal as opposed to electricity; or that a railroad would be more economically efficient than a highway between two locations, or, indeed, that any developed transportation system is economically worthwhile between two given locations? The Austrian argument maintains that it would be epistemologically impossible to rationally determine the economic uses toward which scarce resources should be put without the knowledge-disseminating character of spontaneously generated market prices to guide the enterprise's production plan. The problem it faces is one of deciding which use must be pursued and which others sacrificed. Indeed it is an eminently economic, rather than technological, problem.[10]

Self-managed socialism may theoretically rely (as neoclassical economics does) on consumer goods prices to impute value upwards through the capital structure, but this grants too much to the power of prices in expressing value and allocating scarce resources. It misidentifies the nature of the information that prices convey. In the standard model, prices are thought to not only assist the decision-maker in overcoming what would otherwise be an infinite number of production alternatives. Equilibrium prices also reduce the production process to a single, objectively determined point.

This essentially ignores problems of knowledge transmission because it assumes that an enterprise (self-managed or capitalist) produces according to a given production function and given prices of the factors of production and output. This changes the economic problem into a merely technical one. In the dynamic world outside the theoretical fiction of economic equilibrium, however, prices fail to render values, preferences, and costs unambiguous and objective.[11] The assumption of complete knowledge of the relevant factors, production functions, and equilibrium prices does not solve the knowledge problem, but in fact obscures it.[12] The real issue is precisely how enterprise managers learn to produce one good over another, which combinations of resources to use, how to produce at lowest cost, and so on.

The economic theory of self-managed socialism does not explain the process by which the appropriate knowledge is conveyed. Horvat seems to limit the knowledge dimension to mere data: "The development of economic statistics, economic analysis, and the technology of gathering, processing, and distributing information enabled economic decision makers to obtain incomparably more relevant information than previously," writes Horvat. "Insofar as the market represented an information system," he claims, "this technological progress meant the perfection of the market" (1982: 337). In other words:

There were two aspects to this improvement: (a) up-to-date and comprehensive economic statistics offered economic decision makers complete information about the economic situation, without delay (whereas the old market gave partial information belatedly); and (b) modern forecasting methods permitted a reduction of uncertainty about future wants, and thus former *ex post* decisions were elevated to *ex ante* decisions. Together, they meant that economic decision makers obtained a rather complete collection of the parameters important in making correct decisions; that is, those that would lead to the production of precisely those commodities that could be sold. We can call such improvement of the operation of the market by *organized information diffusion* among economic decision makers an improvement in the "invisible hand." The *enormously increased speed and precision of information gathering and processing*, made possible by electronic computers, has also substantially improved the "visible hand." (pp. 337-38)

Now we are in a position to better understand Horvat's nod to Hayek when Horvat remarked that "The market is a mechanism for communicating information" (p. 200).

But Horvat misunderstands Hayek's knowledge problem argument. Hayek had always been clear that the fundamental problem is not the transmission of mere economic data:

In the traditional treatment of equilibrium analysis [one assumes] that the data, in the form of demand schedules representing individual tastes and technical facts, are equally given to all individuals and that their acting on the same premises will somehow lead to their plans becoming adapted to each other. That this does not really overcome the difficulty created by the fact that one person's actions are the other person's data, and that it involves to some degree circular reasoning, has often been pointed out. What, however, seems so far to have escaped notice is that this whole procedure involves a confusion of a much more general character, of which the point just mentioned is merely a special instance, and which is due to an equivocation of the term "datum." The data which here are supposed to be objective facts and the same for all people are evidently no longer the same thing as the data which formed the starting-point for the tautological transformations of the Pure Logic of Choice. There "data" meant those facts, and only those facts, which were present in the mind of the acting person, and only this *subjective interpretation* of the term "datum" made those propositions necessary truths. "Datum" meant given, known, to the person under consideration. But in the transition from the analysis of the action of an individual to the analysis of the situation in a society the concept has undergone an insidious change of meaning. (1937: 38-39; emphasis added; also cf. Hayek 1968)

The market process transmits much more than statistical data; if that were all, then indeed it could be foreseeably replaced in the future with a suitably developed computer, and perhaps even the fully participatory ideal espoused by Marx himself would be possible. But the market is not a technological process. The crux of the problem of conveying and using knowledge rests within the capital structure itself—it is a problem of intertemporal coordination—and is therefore inextricably tied to the ownership of the material factors of production and not simply to the values of consumer goods.[13] The discovery procedure of markets is anarchic, unplanned and undesigned. It rests squarely upon "private" control of the means of production.[14]

Here the significance of a production plan points far beyond the narrow context which is within the control of the enterprise, and the informational role of prices to supplement more conventional forms of dialogue becomes crucial. A market price acts as a common "signpost" (Lachmann 1971: 49), to orient the separate plans of owners of capital. In particular, it allows those within an enterprise, using their limited and tacit knowledge of their particular horizon, to integrate their timely production plans in the complex structure of the community of producers as a whole. The economic feasibility of their separate plans is tested through the higgling and haggling of the marketplace, where each producer's wealth is at stake. Inevitably some plans will clash, forcing enterprises to adjust their respective plans (substituting one resource for another, revising their expectations concerning demands and supplies of inputs and outputs, and so forth) until a generally undesigned and remarkably integrated pattern emerges.

The market order is thus coordinated *ex post*. Horvat apparently fails to understand that the attempt to duplicate (let alone surpass) the complexity of the market order through *ex ante* planning requires that the necessary knowledge that is distributed throughout millions of individual minds cannot be effectively concentrated in the offices of a planning bureau. Private property in the means of production, and the market prices which emerge from the unhampered exchanges of the means of production, effectively use the bits and pieces of knowledge scattered in the form of skills and contextual know-how among individuals throughout society. It allows, for example, one enterprise to produce steel, another refrigerators, and still others groceries to fill the refrigerators, without members of any given enterprise having to plan or even comprehend the entire process, from the extracting of the iron ore to the farming of the produce. Spontaneous market prices allow individual producers to employ their own knowledge *and* overcome the limitations of their immediate contexts by guiding them through what would otherwise be a bewildering throng of technical possibilities. In this way individual, competing producers offer a greater opportunity for discovering unknown or more efficient combinations of resources than would be possible by a group of planners.

The exchanges of past and present producers and consumers inform a potential enterprise of the economic rationality of its production plan through market price signals. "In abbreviated form, by a kind of symbol," Hayek writes, "only the most essential information is passed on and passed on only to those concerned." The dispersed knowledge of producers and consumers from all sectors of the economy impart usable knowledge to relevant parties in the form of a price signal, a signal which allows one to judge the likelihood that using one resource over another would be more profitable and thus more economically efficient. (An enterprise that contemplates mass-producing refrigerators, for example, will not even consider using a gold or silver construction, even though they may be more durable or aesthetically pleasing than sheet metal, because the relative prices of those resources discourage their consideration as relevant inputs in that particular context.) Market prices supplement one's knowledge in a concrete context by communicating to the entrepreneur in a wholly practical form the differential knowledge of others in their respective contexts.[15]

Moreover, as Hayek argued in *The Road to Serfdom*, the logical implications of socially owned means of production point toward centralized planning and, consequently, a privileged interpretation of economic values. Members of a planning bureau will try to assume the role of a final arbitrator of value. This tension is apparent in the practice of self-managed socialism in Yugoslavia, particularly after the 1974 reforms, to which we now turn.

TENSIONS IN YUGOSLAV PRACTICE

By placing ownership into the hands of "society," rather than individual capitalists or state socialist bureaucrats, and giving workers the right to manage the means of production, *radičko samoupravljanje*, workers' self-management in Yugoslavia, was expected to turn Stalinism on its head. Workers were promised an end to the alienation caused by massive state bureaucracy. Power and control promised to shift from the state to the workers, with the LCY (the League of Yugoslav Communists) serving as their guide. Society was to be rationalized by making the workers' democratic council the fundamental planning unit. Rather than centralized, command planning, Yugoslav society was to be planned from the bottom up. Ultimately, the state was expected to wither away.

Yugoslavia's 1974 constitution underscores the utopian nature of self-managed socialism. Yugoslavia passed through several previous constitutions, enacted in 1946, 1953, and 1963. Although the 1963 constitution was expected to last quite a long time, pressure from the radical left to combat a growing technocracy in the so-called self-managed enterprises brought about amendments in 1967, 1968, and 1971. The 1963 constitution was replaced outright in 1974. Each constitutional change promised to establish further a general system of socialist self-management, one that goes beyond workers' self-management to include self-managed decision-making councils in every walk of life—social, political, and economic. Not only were production processes to be self-managed. So, too, were all aspects of civil society, including culture, the arts, and the sciences. The Yugoslav interpretation of Marx called for an inalienable right among people to manage social resources, one which allows each worker-citizen to associate with other worker-citizens by forming basic production and political units. And the 1974 constitution promised, alas, a smooth and complete blueprint of the *dogovor* economy, the agreement economy, among all spheres of Yugoslav life.[16]

This goal requires, according to the constitution, the full operation of "social ownership" (*društvena svojina*), as opposed to private or state ownership. Only social ownership is considered to be most consistent with Marx's project of de-alienation and comprehensive, democratic planning among associated producers. In the words of a Yugoslav ideologist, "Social ownership banishes all forms of exploitation, monopolistic appropriation and control over the means of production and products of social labour, encourages a rapid development of productive forces and creates the prerequisites for the implementation of Marx's idea about the association of free producers in a communist society" (Stanić 1980: 178-79). The Basic Principles of the Constitution state that

Social ownership of the means of production and other resources shall ensure that everyone becomes integrated, under equal conditions, into associated labour working with social resources, and that, by realizing his right to work with social resources, and on the basis of his own labour, he earns income for the satisfaction of this [sic] personal and common needs. (p. 58)[17]

Social ownership breaks from hierarchical command planning and instead allows for decentralized, participatory planning, as stated in Article 72:

Organizations of labour, self-managing communities of interest and other self-managing organizations and communities shall adjust their working and developing plans and programmes to the plans and programmes of other self-managing organizations and communities with which they have specific common interests and aims which stem from their cooperation and mutual interdependence in social reproduction and which they determine on the basis of self-management agreements. (p. 122)

"Social ownership" was designed to abolish alienation stemming from private and state ownership. According to the constitution, it is outright non-ownership:

Since no one has the right of ownership over social means of production, nobody—not socio-political communities, nor organizations of associated labour, nor groups of citizens, nor individuals—may appropriate on any legal-property grounds the product of social labour or manage and dispose of the social means of production and labour, or arbitrarily determine conditions for distribution.

Man's labour shall be the only basis for the appropriation of the product of social labour and for the management of social resources. (p. 59; cf. Rus 1986)

Social ownership provided the basis for the Party to radically decentralize the self-managed enterprise, apparently in order to reduce the likelihood of technocracy and abuse by managerial personnel. The basic organization of associated labor (BOAL) became the fundamental politico-economic unit, or social planning unit, in Yugoslav society. The 1974 constitution and the 1976 Act of Associated Labor mandated workers in every self-managed enterprise to form democratic councils on the basis of common tasks they shared within the firm. Depending on the type of enterprise, a single self-managed firm may be composed of a couple BOALs to dozens of BOALs. Each BOAL in any given firm would be considered a viable planning unit in itself, capable of generating revenues and earning income. Each BOAL would coordinate its activities with every other BOAL in the enterprise through a series of compactual agreements. Essentially, a self-managed enterprise (the *radna organizacija*, or work organization) is simply the framework within which these individual BOALs interact.[18] Self-managed firms would then coordinate their plans with other self-managed firms through similar compactual and contractual agreements, but at this level the agreements would be reached by councils composed of delegates elected by their respective BOALs.

Hence the notion of the "agreement economy." All decisions in the enterprise would be formed democratically among the various councils that compose each enterprise. Inter-enterprise coordination would be provided through discursive, democratic process as well.

In 1978, over 19,000 BOALs were established in the Yugoslav enterprises. By 1980, over 108,000 BOALs, work communities of associated labor, and self-management communities of interest had been implemented. Their number exceeded 122,000 by 1984.[19] The blueprint was now in place for a decentralized, democratic and humane approach to socialist economic planning. Yugoslavia would finally be planned from the bottom up, as opposed to the top down. The basic planning cell would be the workers' council, rather than an etatist central planning board of the Soviet variety.

As I discussed in the previous chapter, the property rights economists argued that the Yugoslav path to worker control was destined for economic inefficiency because of poor investment incentives. To the extent that the real existing Yugoslav enterprise engages in self-investment, the working collective tends to use long-term loans to finance short-term investment projects. In this way, incumbent workers may enjoy a greater flow of income in the near future while postponing the costs of that decision onto future generations of workers. It goes without saying that the long run effects of such investment policy is extremely damaging to economic growth and stability, and Yugoslavia's present crisis can at least be partly explained by the disincentive effects of the working collectives.[20]

But the explanation for the present crisis goes deeper than that. Yugoslavia has been riddled with contradictions between decentralization and centralization, *de jure* social ownership and *de facto* private (or Party?) ownership, workers' self-management of enterprise and undeniable Communist Party power over crucial enterprise decisions. Economic and political relationships in Yugoslavia have constantly pushed and pulled in two opposing directions, toward an atomistic, chaotic anarchy on the one hand, and toward a totalitarian struggle for power on the other. Yugoslavia has become an exemplary case of the inherent tension between Market and Plan, of which very capable studies have been written.[21]

Neither appropriately decentralized nor fully and comprehensively planned, the Yugoslav system nevertheless preserves the worst elements of these two contradictory extremes.[22] Yugoslavia has been trapped within an *anarcho-stalinism* of sorts.

LIMITS TO DECENTRALIZATION

Consider, for example, the mandated introduction of BOALs into the self-managed enterprises. Over 34,500 BOALs were in place by 1984. Yugoslavia, in principle, had been decomposed into 34,500 basic planning cells. Since the number of plans is at least equal to the number of BOALs (cf. Babić 1980: 8), worker-managers were officially responsible for the coordination of 34,500 interdependent plans. If we add to this figure the number of higher-order councils involved in the coordination process—the work communities of associated labor, the associations of organizations of associated labor, the self-management communities of interest, etc.—the number of planning subjects in Yugoslavia totalled over 122,000 in 1984. The task of exchanging useful economic information was nothing short of impossible. How were they to develop an orderly, coherent, general plan without a spontaneous market process and scarcity-based prices?

The BOAL's *de jure* status as the basic planning unit may have appealed well to the Marxist ideal, especially when compared to the opposite extreme of the all-powerful central planning bureau of the Stalinist model. Decentralization had, however, gone too far.[23] Each move toward *de jure* decentralization of economic decision-making brought about a *de facto* recentralization of political power and LCY influence over all walks of life. By carving society up into arbitrary political and economic units, the Party ensured that it would not have to give up its position of power. Article 72 of the constitution authorized state compulsion in order to coordinate plans and settle conflicts of interest among the multitude of workers' councils:

If the social plan lays down, on the basis of jointly determined interests and aims of development, that the fulfillment of specific tasks is indispensable for social reproduction, and if the organizations of associated labour or other self-managing organizations and communities have not been able to ensure by agreement resources and other necessary conditions for their fulfillment, an obligation to pool resources for the purpose can be introduced by legislation, in conformity with the constitution, and other measures prescribed for the purpose of fulfillment of these tasks. (p. 124)

Moreover, Articles 75–77 obligate the BOALs and other self-management organizations and communities to supply the Social Accountancy Service in Belgrade with all of their bookkeeping accounts, records, transactions, statistics and so on, while Article 50 mandates that all the organizations of associated labor affiliate with the overarching Yugoslav Chamber of the Economy (*Privredna komora Jugoslavija*) in order to facilitate an orderly coordination of plans.

Officially, the chambers have

no elements of power, superiority and control. They are not organizations intended to manage and control the self-management industries, but instead, they stand for the broadest and special form of associating the industries, in the scope of which the industries have the opportunity and obligation to reconcile special, i.e. mutual, as well as joint and general interests. (Simić and Žikić 1987: 12)

The procedure, however, has been very different in practice. The chamber system has failed to reconcile individual, contradictory plans and revise them into a coherent whole. It, too, has been used as a vehicle for state intervention: "Experience of the chambers, especially that of the Yugoslav Chamber of Economy, shows that they have not been involved in a proper way in the operations and activities associated with economic policy making and adjustment of all interests in the industries and the society as a whole" (Simić and Žikić 1987: 13). Though officially a clearing house for information and center of rational economic coordination, the Chamber had instead become an organ of state power: "The expanding etatist approach to the management of the economy has quite unnecessarily involved the Chamber in the so-called daily issues or current economic measures, dragging it away from its active role in the resolution of national economic problems and from its other functions" (p. 13).

In addition, day-to-day decision-making in the Yugoslav enterprise is also influenced through the informal, though powerful, political *aktiv*. The *aktiv* is an organization composed solely of Party members which forms a critical link between the self-managed enterprise and other socio-political organizations. It "assists" the enterprise in important activities such as securing bank loans, construction permits, more favorable prices for inputs, and higher prices for their output. Enterprises must rely upon the *aktiv* to secure valuable scarce resources for their everyday production decisions.[24]

Mihailo Marković had claimed in the early 1970s that "The fundamental lesson which could be drawn from the Yugoslav experience is that self-management by no means should be identified with decentralization and that a local, atomized, disintegrated system of self-management cannot seriously challenge the power of bureaucracy" (1974: 234). Marković held out hope that the 1974 constitution and its integrated blueprint of socialist self-management would eventually destroy the state bureaucracy (1974: 238-39; cf. Supek 1971: 257). It never happened. The Communist Party failed to give up its grip on the system.[25]

MARX'S LEGACY

At his keynote address to the 17th Session of the Central Committee of the LCY, Stipe Šuvar asked fellow LCY members why Yugoslav self-management cannot break the tension between centralization and decentralization after decades of development. Suvar's statement is worth quoting at length:

The past thirty years, since the adoption of the LCY Programme, have been marked by our efforts to emerge from the stage of state socialism. All our efforts, in which milestones have been the LCY Programme, the 1965 economic reform, the constitutional reform of 1971–1974, the model for the political system provided at the 11th Congress in Edvard Kardelj's work, *Democracy and Socialism*, the Long-Term Programme of Economic Stabilization, and the Decisions of the 13th LCY

Congress and stands taken at the LCY Conference [May 1988], have been aimed at further elaborating this original model for our revolution and at channelling the organized social energies of our society to realize them. The past three or four decades have seen a life-and-death struggle between state socialism and the forces of self-management waged over the character of production relations and the lines along which they should change. Society developed rapidly, but today all the postponed crises and earlier mistakes have caught up with us, and society is in the throes of a profound structural crisis. In other words, today's crisis is the culmination of all the social contradictions that have been building up over all these years. In the meantime, considerable confusion has been created in people's minds; there are many ideological misconceptions and illusions, and attempts to cover up the real situation. Today's serious crisis in our society is the product of all the crises of yesterday, and for this reason it is all the more severe and disruptive. If there was nationalism in the past today's nationalism is its consummate expression; if there was bureaucracy in the past, today's bureaucracy is totally hidebound and unproductive; if there was demagoguery and attempts to pool [sic] the wool over people's eyes by false promises of homogeneous communities, the examples we see today far exceed anything from the past. In effect, the position of the creative strata of society which have been pushed into the background, and the status of workers, peasants and the vast majority of the intelligentsia are the best gauge of how much power has been concentrated in the hands of bureaucratic and technocratic forces in the past few decades.

This situation demands complete and concrete answers, above all to the creative forces in society, as to *why they are in such a plight, who put them there, and how they can remedy it. This is the meaning of what it is to be the vanguard.* Finally, it is high time that we resolve the dilemma of whether this is the result of a crisis of theory and an imperfect system, or whether it is the result of poor implementation and incompetent people. (Šuvar 1988: 7-8)

This crisis of Yugoslav socialism—the "life-and-death struggle between statism and self-management"—is predictable from the Mises-Hayek framework. Unable to overcome the knowledge problem that results from a turn to social ownership, Yugoslav self-management failed to break with a totalitarian polity. Marković's lament that "It is possible to have a decentralized but perfectly statist bureaucratic society" (1986: 162) surely rings true in light of four decades of Yugoslav experience. The crisis is not simply the result of poor implementation, political and economic incompetence, or an insincerity among the LCY vanguard and cadres. It is the contemporary manifestation of Marxism's struggle between meaningful workers' self-management and rational comprehensive planning. Both goals have, predictably, remained outside the reach of the Yugoslav peoples.

NOTES

1. It is less clear that Vanek's model faces a tension, if only because it is intended to be a general theory of the self-managed system and not a model of socialist

planning as such. For the greater part of his study, Vanek develops the formal theory of a self-managed market system, which replaces the traditional neoclassical firm with a labor-managed firm. Vanek attempts to show that the labor-managed firm could perform just as well (if not better) than the capitalist twin without having to rely upon economic planning. The supportive structures for cooperatives in the market economy can be voluntarily organized institutions (such as the Federation of Southern Cooperatives in the United States or the *Caja Laboral Popular* in the Mondragon group). In the socialist variant (which is briefly discussed) the supportive structure becomes much more comprehensive and may be responsible for full external financing and investment planning for enterprises using state-owned means of production (see Vanek 1970: ch. 15).

2. Planning in Horvat's theory thus goes well beyond indicative planning (cf. pp. 333-34).

3. Horvat argues that "self-management is behaviorally incompatible with private or collective ownership. It requires social ownership." (1982: 456).

4. Of the early 1960s political and economic reforms Mihailo Marković writes:

The basic relatively attractive elements of the new social contract were: strong emphasis on particular national interests, market competition, a call to the "able ones" to get rich, the so-called "opening to the world" (which meant taking loans from Western banks, free flow of imported goods, indiscriminate consumption, free travel and work in the capitalist West). This new social contract divided the working class, quickly generated a new middle class, produced a deep economic and moral crisis, dealt an almost mortal blow to the project of integral self-government—but it saved the system of *nomenclatura* and restored political bureaucracy. (1986: 167)

5. In fact, this complaint was voiced in Yugoslavia. As Schrenk et al. say of the Yugoslav trade sector during the 1960s:

This growing concentration of control—over what in theory were socially owned financial resources in the trade sector—was regarded to be a violation of the principle of self-management. Workers at other stages of production were being deprived of part of their contribution to the total value of output—to the "surplus value" in Marxian terminology—and their right to participate in its allocation. (1979: 29)

6. While Horvat and others typically consider Yugoslavia's 1965 reform to have launched a "laissez-faire" era, that label is far from descriptive. Although greater market exchange was officially introduced, there still persisted a tremendous degree of *ad hoc* state intervention in the market process. For example, the prices of 90 percent of industrial products remained frozen through the 1960s; the prices of "necessary goods" were fixed by the Federal Executive Council; the state set ceiling prices for "basic" industrial goods; and import quotas were enforced to manipulate prices of goods not subject to direct price control (see Prout 1985: 164-67).

7. Horvat claims that the choice between markets and planning "is not either/ or." He continues: "Then, perhaps, a combination of the two—a sort of mixed economy? That would imply an eclecticism for which there is no need" (p. 332).

8. Claus Bislev argues, for example, that "the market would still play an important role in expressing the consumption preferences of individual consumers, resulting in a broad scale of preferences, and serving as the basis for central planners as well as enterprises" (1985: 393).

9. For example, Hayek's former student Ludwig Lachmann writes that

The heterogeneity which matters is here, of course, not physical heterogeneity, but heterogeneity in use. Even if, at some future date, some miraculous substance were invented, a very light metal perhaps, which it was found profitable to substitute for all steel, wood, copper, etc., so that all capital equipment were to be made from it, this would in no way affect our problem. The real economic significance of the heterogeneity of capital lies in the fact that each capital good can only be used for a limited number of purposes. We shall speak of the multiple specificity of capital goods. (1978: 2)

10. "Technology tells how a given end could be attained by the employment of various means which can be used together in various combinations, or how various available means could be employed for certain purposes," writes Mises. "But it is at a loss to tell man which procedures he should choose out of the infinite variety of imaginable and possible modes of production" (1966: 207; cf. Hayek 1945: 90; Lavoie 1985a: 53-54).

11. "Costs may be taken to have some objective measurability at the margin in full market equilibrium when all economic actors are permitted to adjust their consumptions and resource supplies to take account of market prices," observes Karen Vaughn, "but the minute we move out of equilibrium or away from freely adjusting markets, choice-influencing costs take on a more subjective content, and there is less uniformity in individual evaluations of foregone opportunities" (1980a: 711). Also see Buchanan (1969: ch. 3) on this fundamentally subjective element of cost.

12. Writes Israel Kirzner:

One does not "solve" the problem of dispersed knowledge by *postulating* prices that will smoothly generate dovetailing decisions. Dispersed knowledge is precisely the reason for the very realistic possibility that market prices at a given date are *unable* to clear markets and to ensure the absence of wasted resources. The truth is that the market *does* possess weapons to combat (if not wholly conquer) the problem of dispersed knowledge. These weapons are embodied in the workings of the price system, but *not* in the workings of a hypothetical system of equilibrium prices. (1984: 415)

13. It almost seems that Horvat recognizes this, for he does argue that central planners must exogenously determine the appropriate interest rate (1982: 276) and the optimum rate of investment (pp. 344-47). But he offers little explanation of how this is to be rationally accomplished in a dynamic system.

14. As G. Warren Nutter wrote: markets without property is a "grand illusion" (1983: ch. 13).

15. Private ownership of the means of production allows for spontaneously formed prices for those means of production, and thus competing interpretations as to the values of scarce resources. The exchange of money represents not only one's commitment to a definite plan of action, but an interpretation of the profitability or economic efficiency of that production plan. Competition among economic rivals for the means of production exposes, over time, the underlying scarcities of capital goods and their relatively efficient uses. Because the market process allows for an overwhelmingly large number of competing interpretations over the value of economic goods, it ultimately leads to a high level of anonymity concerning those values.

16. See Prychitko (1990a) for an account of the history of reforms in Yugoslavia. More detailed examinations of the Yugoslav system are provided by Lydall (1986)

and Prout (1985).

17. All references to the 1974 Yugoslav constitution are based on the English-language edition. See *The Constitution of the Socialist Federal Republic of Yugoslavia* Belgrade, 1974 (Ljubljana: Dopisna Delavska Univerza, n.d.).

18. Cf. Horvat:

> If Self-management is to be really meaningful, it must result in direct decision making. For that, a firm—a work organization—has to be broken into constituent units characterized by technological and economic unity of the work process, by autonomous organization of work, by direct management, and by direct distribution of income. The firm appears as a federation of basic organizations of associated labor. (1976: 39)

19. *Yugoslavia 1945-1985: Statistical Overview* (Beograd: Federal Statistical Office, 1989), p. 69.

20. Svetozar Pejovich has recently argued that his predictions (inflation, low savings, high unemployment, and serious liquidity crises) has been observed in Yugoslavia: "Each and every one of these predictions," he writes, "has turned out to be correct" (1984: 431; cf. 1990: 127-131). Yet Horvat, in his bid "Farewell to the Illyrian Firm," concludes that the predictions are simply wrong. He argues, for example: "In Yugoslavia there is a chronic tendency to *overinvestment*—not underinvestment—and that is explained by reduced risk and the availability of investment finance" (1986: 25; cf. 1982: 251). Horvat does not tell us, however, that the reason for Yugoslavia's chronic malinvestment stems precisely from the Furubotn-Pejovich-Vanek effect that workers have little incentive for self-finance. The state in Yugoslavia has thus assumed the responsibility of investment by taxing enterprises in order to force investment. See Bičanić (1989).

21. Contemporary studies of Yugoslavia's "life and death struggle" with statism and self-management have rediscovered the contradictions in the visions of former socialist radicals and revolutionaries. But they seem to overlook contradictions in Marx's writings. For example, Ellen Turkish Comisso's (1979) fine empirical study of a Yugoslav self-managed enterprise interprets the Yugoslav tension as a synthesis of "two complementary yet contradictory schemas of workers' control" (p. 3): the centralism of Antonio Gramsci and the anarchism of P. J. Proudhon. Comisso interprets contemporary Yugoslavia as being tugged in the two antagonistic directions promoted by Gramsci and Proudhon. More recently, Rudi Supek (1989; cf. Supek 1971) seemed to improve upon Comisso's argument by using Occam's razor to cut Gramsci out of the explanation. Supek argues that the tension in Yugoslav self-management can be traced back to Proudhon alone, as Proudhon struggled between notions of freedom (decentralization) and equality (centralization) in his vision of mutualist socialism.

But, more than Gramsci, Proudhon, or any other revolutionary, one cannot overlook the fact that the Yugoslav ideal of self-managed socialism is most indebted to Karl Marx, as I discussed in chapters 2 and 3. And I believe that the tension between statism and self-management under "real existing" socialism in Yugoslavia can profitably be traced to an inherent tension in Marx's life-work. The Yugoslav crisis seems to be fundamentally a crisis of theory and system, a crisis which has its roots in Marx.

22. Daniel Guerin, who held hope for the radically decentralized, anarchic spirit

of Yugoslav self-management, complained of extreme state and party intervention in Yugoslav practice. Says Guerin:

These good intentions are far from being carried out in practice.... [S]elf-management is coming into being in the framework of a dictatorial, military, police state whose skeleton is formed by a single party. At the helm there is an authoritarian and paternalistic authority which is beyond control and above criticism. The authoritarian principles of the political administration and the libertarian principles of the management of the economy are thus quite incompatible. (1970: 146)

23. Stojanović writes that

The most important legacy of de-statization was the development of self-management *at the workplace*. It was first instituted in the economy and then broadened to other areas as well. In practice, however, self-management has been limited to problems of production and distribution. Genuinely political questions are tacitly reserved for the organizations of the LCY, particularly its leadership.

In the vertical organization of society there were also created a series of forms and institutions which were termed "self-managing"—assemblies of delegates from the commune, republic, and federal levels; communities of interest; and diverse associations and chambers. Since there are no *real* elections for these bodies, all this is merely *formal* self-management. Were such elections to take place, the resulting system, encompassing some two million delegates of various sorts, would be democratic almost second to none. (1981: 80)

24. Other Party influences on the allegedly autonomous, self-managed enterprise abound. The LCY legally required individuals to pass "moral-political fitness" tests as a way to place disciplined cadres into all important posts (Stojanović 1981: 83, 96 n. 45). Also see Carter (1982: ch. 13).

25. As Najdan Pašić laments:

the ideology of self-management is, in terms of its consequences, an ideology of self-destruction. To put it simply, every important practical step towards realizing the proclaimed long-term interests of a consistently developed system of self-management, capable of self-reproduction without the arbitrary intervention of the political power of the state has unavoidably clashed with the position of the party apparatus, if the latter remained the integral and most influential part of the existing power structure. Thus, all radical demands, even measures of a more modest scope, aimed at reducing and finally eliminating bureaucratic paternalism over self-management-based relations and institutions have met inevitably with spontaneous or deliberate resistance within the powerful stratum of professional rulers, including part of the Party leadership. (1988: 79-80)

Also Laura Tyson remarks that, although the BOALs were supposed to decentralize decision-making,

An important centralizing force was operating simultaneously with these decentralizing trends, however—namely, the consolidation of the LCY and the broadening of its direct policy role in many areas of economic activity. In the new institutional system, the LCY was restored as the final authority over all decision-makers. (1980: 8)

Also see Baumgartner, Burns, and Sekulić (1979: 110-17).

CHAPTER 6 _____

Worker Cooperatives Within a Market Process: Lessons from the Cooperage Cooperatives of Minneapolis, 1864–1929

INTRODUCTION

The growing interest in the viability of participatory and self-managed work organizations in fundamentally market-based systems has inspired some studies of producer cooperatives in American history. The work of Shirom (1972) and especially Jones (1977; 1979; 1982) have made valuable contributions toward our understanding of the extent and nature of producer cooperation in the United States. Understandably, the question of the viability of these cooperatives within a capitalistic economy becomes a significant issue, not least because of its relevance to the debate over the feasibility of self-managed socialism and the problem of knowledge.

Throughout this book I have considered workers' cooperation largely within a socialist setting, in which the means of production are socially owned, and activities coordinated by a comprehensive plan or a combination of plan and limited market exchange. I have been critical of the economic rationality of the socialist models of workers' cooperation because they do not seem to adequately answer the knowledge problem. From a comparative systems perspective, the viability of worker cooperatives may be greater in a market system based upon private (or joint) ownership of the means of production as opposed to state or social ownership. Pockets of worker cooperatives may be reconciled with an unrestrained market (the spontaneous exchange of the means of production) if indeed the market process imparts much more useable knowledge to a cooperative enterprise than would a planning office or statistical bureau.

But can cooperatives keep apace with the innovations and technological swings of the market? Supporters of traditional forms of business organization argue that cooperatives will generally try to resist technological change, preserve the privileges of workers at the expense of market coordination, or simply fail to compete with boss shops or corporate hierarchies.

Economists as ideologically diverse as Yugoslavia's Branko Horvat and the Austrian school economist Murray Rothbard claim that history demonstrates the infeasibility of workers' cooperatives in a market system. Horvat (1982: 457) argues that "the history of British and American cooperatives has been quite unimpressive. And nowhere else have producer cooperatives attained more than negligible importance." "Producers' cooperatives, in a capitalist environment," he concludes, "turned out to be a failure" (p. 128; cf. 1975a: 21). Rothbard, an "anarcho-capitalist," maintains: "Empirically, it has been demonstrated time and again that cooperatives cannot compete successfully against stock-owned companies, especially when both are equal before the law" (1970: 123; cf. p. 213, n. 88).

But these beliefs are unfounded. Derek Jones (1977) identifies 421 worker cooperatives established between 1791–1939 in the United States alone, and thus demonstrates that the experience of producers' cooperation in a market system is not as meager as earlier studies suggested. Peter Jay sums up the experience as follows:

> in very broad terms it leaves an impression that producer co-operatives have tended to be small, to be short-lived and to have difficulty surviving in the prevailing environment, although there are some important exceptions.
>
> But this evidence has to be interpreted with great care, if morals are to be drawn about the viability of market socialism. The American evidence and literature have been usefully examined by Derek C. Jones. . . . He throws considerable doubt on the conventional view that American producer co-operatives failed through inherent weaknesses. (1980: 39-40)

Jones's (1977) statistical overview illustrates (contrary to the general understanding of the American experience) that many cooperatives survived for more than two decades.

By taking an "interpretive turn" in order to "get behind the data" of history that Jones and others have carefully, and fruitfully, presented, I shall use the case study method in this chapter to illustrate the comparative economic systems issues of worker cooperatives within a market context. I shall try to show in what particular respects an historically significant group of worker cooperatives succeeded and in what respects they failed.

Specifically, I shall examine the group of cooperage (barrel-making) co-operatives formed in Minneapolis near the turn of the century. These cooperatives are quite relevant to the issue at hand, for they faced extremely competitive market conditions, and, though some eventually went out of business, others adapted to the changing demands of the market and survived for a number of years.

WHAT CONSTITUTES SUCCESS?

Jones recognizes that interpreting the success of a cooperative venture is no simple matter:

Is five years really a sufficiently long period to appropriately assess an organization's economic viability? Is this assessment done properly by looking at the ability of the firm to generate a surplus during the period? Perhaps a longer time period is needed and one that employs diverse measures of economic performance, rather than relying solely on profitability. It may also be that the evaluation of workplace democracy must include more than an examination of the opportunities available to members. The proportion of the workforce that assume [sic] membership status must also be considered. Furthermore, perhaps it should be explicitly stated that the opportunities available to members be on an equal basis. (1979: 356)

The cooperage cooperatives of Minneapolis are a case in point. They have been considered among the most successful experiments in workers' co-operation within a market system. Of the scores of American producer cooperatives launched in the latter half of the 1800s, one of the most long-lived groups emerged among the journeymen coopers of Minneapolis. One of the cooperatives, the North Star Barrel Company, was organized in 1877 and lasted until 1929, almost 53 years.

Several economists noted the significance of the cooperage cooperatives. The American economist Arthur T. Hadley said that "of American attempts in productive cooperation the most conspicuous instance has been furnished by the coopers of Minneapolis" (1896: 380). Richard T. Ely, among the most respected American economists of the time, argued that "The most remarkable success of co-operative production is found among the coopers of Minneapolis" (1969: 188). Elsewhere he stated that the cooperatives have "as much significance as the Rochdale pioneers" (Ely quoted in Knapp 1969: 42). As late as 1929, S. Howard Patterson recalled of the American experience that even though the record is mixed, "there are such notable exceptions as the Cooperative Barrel Manufacturing Company of Minneapolis" (1929: 461).[1]

Fifty three years is indeed exceptional. But, keeping in mind Jones's perceptive question of just what constitutes success, clearly the fact that the North Star Barrel Company remained in business for that long does not necessarily demonstrate its success as a cooperative entity. To demonstrate success it may prove helpful to look more closely at the details of this case, keeping in mind the theoretical issues raised in the previous chapters.

In order to interpret the degree of success of this market experiment in productive cooperation, the context within which the historical actors oriented themselves needs to be considered in some detail. These contextual factors would include the purposes, goals, and expectations of the journeymen coopers. Contemporary economic research on the cooperage cooperatives (and most other historical cases) has not taken this into account. For example, concerning the issue of what constitutes success, contemporary researchers tend to overlook the following questions: How did the coopers interpret the competitive environment in Minneapolis? What motivated them to leave the boss shops and assume the difficult task of establishing cooperatives? How did they view the use of machinery and unskilled labor? In short, what did they believe cooperation could do for them that could not be achieved in the boss shops? Did cooperation meet their expectations? If we wish to understand this episode in terms of success or failure, we must refer, in part, to the cooperators' intentions.

When we keep in mind the goals of the coopers, it is clear that in many ways the cooperage cooperatives are a worst-possible-case example, for over time many of the cooperative ideals were abandoned, and the cooperages increasingly resembled joint stock companies as opposed to truly cooperative organizations. Why, then, discuss this particular group of cooperatives? After all, excellent studies already exist that demonstrate that cooperatives can effectively compete with market rivals, such as the plywood cooperatives of the Northwest (see Gunn 1984), the San Francisco scavenger cooperatives (see Perry 1978), and the Mondragon network of industrial cooperatives in Spain (see Thomas and Logan 1982; Whyte and Whyte 1988). The cooperage cooperatives warrant consideration *precisely* because they emerged with many strikes against them: the late 1800s initiated the heyday of Taylorism; the skills of the cooper were becoming obsolete through ever-increasing mechanization; the barrel industry as a whole was becoming displaced by more efficient packages such as sacks. And yet the cooperage cooperatives were still partially successful. Given different institutional circumstances there is reason to be optimistic over the future of worker ownership, despite some of the features of the story of the coopers, to which we now turn.

THE CASE OF THE COOPERS

The coopers' cooperatives were part of the great boom in cooperative associations formed during the period from the 1860s to the 1880s. Jones (1979) identifies twenty-eight producers' cooperatives established during the 1860s, fifty-one during the 1870s, and 275 during the 1880s across the country and across industries. They ranged from the foundry cooperatives in New York to the shingle-weaving cooperatives in Washington.

In contrast to earlier attempts to establish utopian cooperatives (such as Owen's New Harmony and the Fourier Societies), the producers' cooperatives of the 1860s–1880s emerged not so much from ideological considerations as from the sporadic employment and unsuccessful strikes that characterized the period. And, as I discussed in chapter 3, they generally received quite an excited welcome from the intellectual community. Many intellectuals gave the impression that the cooperative undertakings were spurred largely by ideological concerns (Richard Ely, proclaimed "There is a determination on the part of the masses to extend triumphant democracy into the business world" [1887: 150]).

The first state cooperative laws were enacted in Michigan (1865), Massachusetts (1866), Pennsylvania (1868), and Minnesota (1870) (see Shaw 1888). As early as 1882, profit-sharing emerged as a way of "partial cooperation," among which the Pillsbury Mills provided a prime example.[2] Cooperation was generally spreading across the country and in the economics literature.

The Knights of Labor, initially organized in 1869 as a secret order and outgrowth of the unsuccessful Garment Cutters Association of Philadelphia, took advantage of the prevailing tendencies toward cooperation and set out on a massive propaganda campaign to encourage cooperative reforms. Jones (1979: 343) counts 200 such cooperatives organized in the 1880s. The Local Assembly of the Knights of Labor intended to "assist members to better their condition, morally, socially, and financially." Cooperation was to replace strikes, for "strikes, at best, only afford temporary relief; and members should be educated to depend upon thorough organization, co-operation, and political action, and, through these, the abolishment of the wage system" (Knights' statement quoted in Wright 1887: 160).[3]

By 1880 the Knights' cooperative fund was derived from monthly fees of a dime per male, a nickel per female member to finance cooperative undertakings, and was to be administered through the General Cooperative Board. The demands placed on the Board were extraordinary, as cooperative concerns sprouted across the country and struggled for their existence.[4]

The first cooperative shop was formed in the spring of 1868, by four journeymen: Chauncey W. Curtis, William H. Reeves, George W. Sargent, and Joseph Combs. Their primary goal was stable wages and employment.[5] In addition, each had the skills of an expert cooper, which he also wished to maintain.[6] As Albert Shaw described it, the coopers "began simply and informally. No organization was necessary. Each owned his kit of tools, and there were no large initial outlays to be made. They rented a small shop that was standing idle, purchased barrel stock in small quantities, and went to work" (1886: 11). As cooperators the four agreed to receive piece-price wages equal to what the other journeymen around town were receiving and divide any residuals on the proportion of the work contributed by each. At the time the mills in Minneapolis were producing a little over 100,000 barrels annually, and the market had its ups and downs. Though Shaw says that the venture was "in every aspect a success," the shop closed a few months later as many of the mills either cut back output or shut down completely. The members accordingly sold their concern and once again worked as journeymen in a local "boss" shop.[7]

Afterward, milling activity in Minneapolis grew rapidly. Close to 200,000 barrels of flour were produced in 1870; by 1873 the number had trebled. The demand for coopers increased accordingly. Wages were relatively stable, if not rising at times, and employment was easy to find, at least early in the period. But the inflowing supply of coopers eventually outpaced the growth in demand. The resulting fall in wages and sporadic employment opportunities for journeymen encouraged an "active hostility" between them and the owners of the boss shops (Shaw 1886: 13-14). Several strikes broke out. The coopers of the Doud and Son boss shop struck in response to a three cent reduction in the price of barrels, which forced the shop to secure coopers from Milwaukee.[8]

Efforts to unionize succeeded in 1874 with the establishment of a coopers' union.[9] But some sixty coopers were thrown out of employment by George H. Christian and Company when it de-unionized two out of its three boss shops. The *St. Paul Dispatch* (August 26, 1874) said the shops were "bound to be loosened from the thraldom of the union, and will here after have nothing to do with guilds, trades, union, etc." C. W. Curtis, along with other union men, tried to renew their contract with Christian and Co. but to no avail.

As a result, Curtis and four others founded the Cooperative Barrel Manufacturing Company in the fall of 1874, and were able to establish a contract with one of the Pillsbury mills in town. They were to supply Pillsbury with 300 to 350 barrels per day.[10] Producing this many barrels for Pillsbury meant that the new cooperative could support a large membership, guided by a rigorous set of by-laws.[11]

The formal organization was thoroughly cooperative: Members were equal shareholders who apportioned "ordinary" profits or losses on the basis of the amount (and presumably the quality) of the barrels completed, while profits or losses stemming from changes in the capital value of the cooperative (such as through fire or changing real estate values), in addition to that directly related to hired help, was apportioned equally among all members. Firing an existing member required a two-thirds vote of all the members, and share transfer was allowed only with the consent of the managerial board. All voting took place on the basis of one person, one vote, as provided by the 1870 Minnesota law that allowed for the formation of cooperative associations.[12] The Board of Managers, (which consisted of the president, treasurer, and three directors) conducted and managed the affairs of the cooperative, and was chosen annually by the shareholders as stipulated in Section 5 of the 1870 state law.

In its first few years of operation, the Cooperative Barrel Company had less than twenty-five members. By 1885 membership swelled to 120. The cooperative's fully paid capital, "being constantly augmented by weekly assessments and issuance of new shares of stock from time to time," amounted to roughly $50,000 (Shaw 1886: 22-3). They enjoyed capital gains largely through an increased value of real estate owned by the cooperative rather than any cost advantages in barrel-making (Shaw 1886: 25; Virtue 1905: 529).

The members of the Cooper's Union went on strike again in 1877 as a result of wage reductions; by November work was "suspended in almost every shop in the city."[13] In October 1877 Curtis, Bachelder, Kenney, and a couple others left the Cooperative Barrel Company to form the North Star Barrel Company, probably in order to compete more successfully with the highly productive boss shops.[14]

The North Star began with $1800 in capital, contributed from eighteen original members each investing in two fully paid shares of stock. The cooperative thrived and membership increased dramatically during the early 1880s. By 1882 it reached 100, its highest figure, as the North Star bought out a competitor, the Liberty Cooperative Barrel Company and absorbed its twenty-six shareholders. At this time the North Star began to occasionally hire eight journeymen coopers. They were paid the same wages as the shareholders of the North Star, but were not recognized as members.[15]

Other rival cooperatives were formed during this period, many due to the strikes in the boss shops, the introduction of machinery, and an over-supplied market for skilled labor. These included the Liberty Barrel Company, which, as mentioned above, arose in June 1879. Though it predicted its operation would continue "for twenty years" (*St. Paul Daily Globe*, June 3, 1879), it was absorbed by North Star in 1882. Hennepin County Barrel Company originated in March, 1880, with twenty-four members contributing $25 each. By February 1881 its membership doubled to fifty. The Excelsior Cooperative Barrel Company was formed in 1880 with twenty-five members, and was later absorbed by the Cooperative Barrel Company in 1881. The Phoenix Barrel Company was formed in March 1881 by journeymen from the Ames Shop (a local boss shop) who lost their jobs when the Ames shop sold some of its assets to the newly formed Hennepin County Barrel Company. Here, thirty charter members each contributed a downpayment of $15 for one $50 share of stock. Later (in

December of that year), the Northwestern Barrel Company was established as a result of a strike among forty journeymen in the Hall and Dann's boss shop. Each of the forty members invested $15 a share.

Success in the market breeds imitation. It appears that all these cooperative shops borrowed the same set of by-laws and formal organization from the successful Cooperative Barrel Company. Indeed, some, such as the Hennepin shop, borrowed them *in toto*, as a way to economize on knowledge (Shaw 1886: 28).

Capital accumulation generally took the form of two or more dollars a week deducted from the piece-price wages of the members.[16] Moreover, the cooperative shops were at no particular disadvantage when it came to generating financial capital. In 1886 the net assets of all the cooperatives amounted to $150,000, of which $118,000 belonged to the Cooperative Barrel Company, the North Star, and the Hennepin County cooperative, and by 1905 the three firms had assets over $160,000 (Virtue 1905: 536). Again much of this was due to the members' entrepreneurial foresight in real estate speculation, as they took advantage of the dramatic increase in the value of real estate they acquired while Minneapolis grew from a village of 2,500 residents in 1860 to 47,000 in 1880, and broke 200,000 in 1900.

It appears that a market existed for the transfer of membership, given the appropriate consent of a cooperative's board of directors (see Shaw 1886: 24, 42). The fact that workers could recuperate the value of their investments upon exiting the cooperative, in addition to this option to sell, allowed the cooperatives' members to get around the difficulties of social property that I discussed in chapter 4.

During the early 1880s, increased milling activity brought in its wake not only more cooperative shops, but also a widespread use of machinery in the cooper shops. By 1880 the Hall and Dann shop completed the "largest barrel factory in the world" (*St. Paul Daily Globe*, December 3, 1880), with a capacity of 6,000 barrels a day; compare this to the Cooperative and North Star shops producing a total of 1,200 and 1,500 barrels a day as late as 1885 (*Daily Minneapolis Tribune*, August 24, 1885). Barrels produced partly by machine were two to three cents cheaper than those made by hand. Even at such a small margin, many of the cooperative shops found it necessary to introduce machines to compete with their more efficient rivals.

While the widespread use of machinery first began in 1874, machinery found its way into a cooperative shop, namely the Hennepin County shop, some eight years later. The Cooperative Barrel Company and the North Star followed later in 1885, at the cost of relatively large reductions in membership. Although this conflicted with the original hopes of achieving stable employment and preserving obsolete skills, it permitted these cooperatives to respond to rapidly changing technology and to continue to compete with the boss shops.

The introduction of machinery greatly increased the number of barrels produced, and actually increased their quality. This would naturally undermine the traditionalist mentality promoted by the old style hand cooper.[17] Coopering was a skill, a handcraft learned through apprenticeships and a tradition that spanned several generations. With the enormous growth in milling activities in the city, the cooperage enterprise had to increase the efficiency of its methods or be replaced by other forms of storage.

The term "cooper shop" came to be replaced by the term "barrel factory," as the Hall and Dann's shop was described above.[18] During the 1880s, technology improved to the point where machines were also capable of completing the barrel. As Coyne mentioned, "When these machines were added to those previously installed, the barrel was completed entirely with the aid of machinery, even to boring the bung hole, and the oldtime cooper as well as the later hooper, or hooper-cooper, became only a memory" (1940: 24).

For a time Luddite thinking prevailed among many coopers. A letter to the editor of the first issue of the *National Coopers' Journal* (May 1885, p. 2) states, for instance, that there were

clouds cast by the cooperage machinery that is surely finding a place in this city to the great disgust of the rank and file coopers. . . . It is no longer a secret that the North Star Barrel Co. have ordered full sets of machinery. . . . The Co-operative Co. have voted machinery. Part of the machinery for the Northwestern Barrel Co. has arrived and is being placed in position, others may follow.

A war between the hand coopers and the machine men seems inevitable. As a cooper and affiliating with coopers your correspondent hopes the hand men may come out on top.

It is interesting that the author of the letter called himself a "cooper" as opposed to the "machine men" of the *cooperative* shops. In fact, however, the coopers in Minneapolis were not the old style hand coopers who never relied upon machinery, though some often promoted this image. Nevertheless, many found the scale of machinery being introduced to be a significant threat to their skilled livelihoods, which undoubtedly went against one of the initial aims of cooperation—securing the current skills of the cooper.[19]

Despite the traditionalist mentality and the initial aspiration to fight against a technologically advancing market, the cooperatives nevertheless succeeded in adopting the new technology, partly because the flexibility of the property rights arrangement allowed for a relatively smooth exit of workers when machinery was inevitably introduced. Shaw observes, for example:

When the introduction of machinery rendered the membership of the Cooperative
Company too large by one-fourth, it was perfectly easy to make adjustment upon
a voluntary basis. Some men preferred to transfer their ownership to other shops
where business happened to be better. Others were glad to take advantage of the
company's offer of full cash payment of capital to set up as merchants in a small
way or as farmers on government or railroad land. In most cases, naturally, men
who withdrew were recent rather than old members, bachelors rather than married
men, and renters rather than owners of homes in the vicinity of the shop. The easy
self-adjustment of membership to the conditions of business in these cooperative
shops is a matter sufficiently noteworthy to justify the illustration. (1886: 24)

Competition was stiff between all the cooperage shops in the city, cooperative and boss shop alike. And the cooperatives that introduced the
technology were surviving. Machines were necessary to increase the productivity of the coopers, which allowed an incumbent shop to maintain a
competitive advantage in the market, as it was now over three times more
expensive to produce barrels by hand rather than machine, and took well
over twice as long.[20] Those shops that would not, or could not, introduce
machines were assured of being weeded out by the market's competitive
process.[21] As the *St. Paul Daily Globe* described it: "Everybody has got
to rustle for business, for the fellows that are left will have to close up
shop or retire on their capital" (September 27, 1885).

Considering the goals of cooperation suggests that a conflict of interests
existed within the cooperative shops: In order for a cooperative shop to
remain in operation, machines were necessary. But in many cases machines
eventually replaced the skilled labor of the coopers with the unskilled labor
of boys; this turned former members into journeymen once again, facing
the journeyman's contingencies of sporadic employment, unstable wages,
and a loss of brotherly solidarity. They were left complaining about the
"machine men" in the city. The original, unattainable hope to preserve
cooperage skills and the stability of employment under such dynamic,
evolving markets was abandoned. The cooperatives had the flexibility,
however, to respond to market signals through merger and the introduction
of machinery. When the Cooperative Barrel Company introduced machines in 1885, its membership decreased from 120 to ninety within a year.
The North Star's membership fell from eighty in 1884 to sixty-five in 1886,
the year following its initial use of machines. Though I have not been able
to find how the membership voted on these issues (in order to determine
the possibility of factions existing among the members), G. O. Virtue
argued that machines may have been used as a weapon by the successful
cooperative shops to get rid of the new members that came about through
merger activities: "Whenever it has become necessary to increase the membership, as in the process of getting rid of a competitor, the problem soon
presented itself of getting rid of that increase" (1905: 538). This is certainly
an issue for further research of the type I have suggested. On the basis of

these preliminary findings, however, I am inclined to say that machines seem to have been the solution. For example, The Hennepin County shop's merger with the Northwestern Barrel Company in 1896 increased Hennepin's membership from sixty to ninety-six; but it fell to sixty-six two years later with further reliance on machine technology. In this way the incumbent member's share of the residual was not dampened, and may have been increased with increased efficiencies in production, while there was also the added benefit of one less market competitor to worry about.

There is little doubt that in this case many cooperatives survived market competition but became, to differing degrees, less cooperative as time passed. Unskilled laborers working for a straight wage, not having any voting rights, replaced many of the skilled coopers, for only coopers were admitted to membership. Virtue remarked in 1905 that "Nearly half the men in the Hennepin shop are non-members: about one-third of the wages paid by the Co-operative Company goes to outsiders. . . . [while] In the North Star 30 non-members are regularly employed, only 3 or 4 of them coopers; and in busy seasons the company employs 25 or 30 journeymen additional" (1905: 538-39).

Not only did the pressure of an extremely competitive barrel industry test the entrepreneurial ability of the cooperative coopers. To make matters more challenging, the industry as a whole was being effectively displaced by a much more efficient package—the sack. This caused the flour barrel industry to change rapidly near the turn of the century. In 1885 there were eleven cooperage shops in Minneapolis, seven of which were cooperative, employing some 600 coopers. By 1904 the number fell to five shops, two boss shops and three cooperatives, employing less than 250 coopers. In an article in the *National Coopers' Journal*, Fred J. Clark (1904) lamented that "boldly standing out in relation to the barrel trade is the fact that sacks are gradually superseding barrels as flour packages. This is particularly emphasized in the case of Minneapolis."[22] In 1889 the Minneapolis coopers sold 2,617.990 barrels, which accounted for 40.3 percent of the total Minneapolis flour output. By 1903 3,129,360 barrels were sold, but this accounted for only 20 percent of the Minneapolis output. Much of the competition stemmed from the Eastern United States, which campaigned for the sack as a better package compared to the barrel: "The Eastern trade is no doubt being 'educated' to buy flour in sacks," said Clark, "and the use of barrels is unquestioningly gradually decreasing."[23]

Worse yet, the market for second-hand barrels began to strongly compete with the new barrel market, as the former enjoyed favorable freight rates. An article by George E. Walsh in a 1905 issue of *Scientific American* (entitled "The Life of a Barrel") argued that the barrel's virtue is that it has "as many lives as a cat": it could be reused again and again. The problem was that this reduced the demand for new barrels. The January 1899 issue of *Barrel and Box* complained that the coopers' unions are continually fighting machine barrels that sell for the highest market price, but take no notice of the second-hand package that is causing more real detriment to the trade than all the machines in the country. . . . the cost of this class of packages is so cheap that they have wrested the trade from the coopers, to such an extent many of them have been compelled to abandon their trade. . . . Viewed from any standpoint taken, this class of traffic is detrimental to the best interests of those engaging in making new work. (p. 34)

That the cooperage cooperatives were able to withstand this competition through the early 1900s is remarkable, especially when one considers that the production of flour in Minneapolis fell from 16.1 million barrels in 1914 to 10.4 million by 1929 (Virtue 1932: 543). The North Star merged with the Cooperative Company in 1918, adding twenty-six members to the North Star for a total of about sixty. Through the 1920s the membership of the North Star declined to twenty-six, mainly due to death and withdrawal of its elderly members. The Hennepin went under before the North Star, in 1928, with thirty-five members, only one under the age of sixty-five. When the North Star finally ceased operations in 1929, it had $106,000 to divide among its twenty-six members, each receiving roughly $4,000.

Thus, there is little doubt that these three cooperative shops were economically successful business entities. Moreover, they exhibited precisely the kind of flexibility required for market coordination. That the cooperatives introduced machinery allowed them to survive through the 1920s; after that, instead of augmenting their machinery to adapt to the changing technology in barrel manufacturing, they essentially switched industries. The Cooperative and North Star enterprises, for example, turned to the production of butter tubs, mainly using the hired labor of young men rather than the skill of the cooper. Admittedly, under these adverse conditions these shops gradually lost their cooperative character. But this occurred over the course of several years. Some of the cooperatives, such as the Cooperative Barrel Manufacturing Company, survived at least a decade in the cooperative format. That is a substantial success in its own right.[24]

Plant and equipment of an increasingly greater scale was necessary for the efficient production of barrels. The cooperatives accordingly introduced machinery to remain in operation, which replaced the skilled labor of the member cooper with the unskilled labor of hired hands. The hope that the cooperative form of business organization would preserve the skills of the cooper and offer a stable means of employment, was proven unrealistic within a dynamic market setting, and consequently abandoned by the members themselves.

RECONSIDERING THE COOPERAGE COOPERATIVES

Jones (1979) raised a fundamental question regarding the criteria we ought to use in historically judging success. One should take into account many factors to evaluate a workers' cooperative: the financial soundness of the cooperative, the opportunities available to workers, the proportion of those enjoying membership status, and so on. One should also consider the less quantifiable aspects of cooperation, such as the reasons why workers would wish to embark upon such an effort in the first place. I have argued that a meaningful notion of success must recognize the motivations and intentions of those who choose to form a cooperative over other productive organizations. In the case of the Minneapolis cooperage cooperatives, my narrative suggests a partial failure in this particular case to achieve and preserve coopering skills and achieve stable employment, apparently one of the original intentions of the cooperators. But they also intended to run profitable firms themselves, to enjoy capital gains and survive the stiff competition from boss shops. Though after a decade or two they increasingly resembled joint-stock companies, they were still economically successful when judged by the market. Indeed, what is remarkable is the fact that the property rights arrangement within the cooperatives allowed for such a degree of flexibility that they could adjust to market conditions which were anything but favorable. Contrary to the typical opinions of the critics, at least this group of cooperatives had no problem securing investment from its members; they introduced new technology; and they were able to compete with the boss shops. Indeed, they outcompeted them in several cases.

No single case study can be used to generalize the whole historical record. That, certainly, is not my intent. I believe the cooperage cooperatives are significant because they were economically successful in a worst-case scenario. They faced adverse, extremely competitive markets. Mechanization was rendering their skills obsolete. Then the barrel-making industry eventually was weeded out by sacks. That the original ideals of the founding members were not fully achieved is no cause for alarm, nor reason to believe cooperatives must degenerate into joint stock companies in an unhampered market process.

NOTES

1. Also see Catlin (1926: 572), Commons and Associates (1926: 76), Ely (1887: 150; 1969: 188), Fetter (1922: 334), Gunn (1984: 30), Jelley (1969: 272), Knapp (1969: 42), Myrick (1895: 138-42), Patterson (1929: 462), Perlman (1937: 56), Stephen (1984: 159), Virtue (1905: 527; 1932: 541, 544), and Watkins (1922: 547). Albert Shaw (1886) provided the first systematic study of the coopers. In a letter to Richard Ely (quoted in Ely 1969: 188-89), Shaw wrote: "I have found a remarkable instance of producer co-operation. I have already begun to collect the data for an economic essay. . . . So far as I am aware, these cooper-shops form the most successful examples of productive cooperation in the world; and yet, if anybody has ever alluded to them in a scientific way, I have never found it out."

Yet, in Joseph G. Knapp and Associates' 607 page book, *Great American Co-*

operators: Biographical Sketches of 101 Major Pioneers in Cooperative Development (1967), none of the men behind the cooperage cooperatives in Minnesota is mentioned. Since Knapp was aware of the cooperages (see Knapp 1969: 42), this may reflect the scarcity of any remaining primary documents of the cooperage enterprises.

2. See Shaw (1886: 65-69). Also see Monroe (1896) for a rather comprehensive study of thirty-three firms which engaged in profit sharing near the turn of the century.

3. The local Minneapolis assemblies # 805 and 3363 consisted entirely of coopers, but the memberships were quite unstable. For instance, #805, while having 128 members at year-end 1879, fell to twenty-four in 1880, twenty-one in 1881, increased to sixty-four in 1882, eighty-six in 1884, and 132 in 1885 (Garlock 1982: 230, 598, 599). Engberg (1941: 373) noted that "Both journeymen and co-operative coopers belonged to the coopers' assembly of the Knights of Labor, but that did not prevent friction from developing between rival groups." I have found no evidence, however, that any of the cooperage cooperatives in Minneapolis were formed under the auspices of the Knights.

4. A quote by the Secretary of the Board of the Knights of Labor (cited in Commons et al. 1926: 436) suggests that most of the cooperative undertakings at this time, especially under the auspices of the Knights of Labor, were quite marginal and doomed to failure. It actually seems that the Co-operative Board, collecting fees in the name of encouraging cooperation, was largely a front to finance the numerous strike activities the Knights had been engaging in at the time, some of which were successful. See Ware's classic study of the Knights (1959: 322-23).

5. According to Shaw, Curtis "believed that if the 'bosses' were dispensed with and the associated mechanics could deal directly with the mills, they would gain both in wages and in the certainty of employment. In the spring of 1868 he persuaded [the others] to join him in a cooperative experiment" (1886: 11).

6. More recent historical studies by Herbert G. Gutman (1976) and David Montgomery (1979) provide a strong case that cooperative efforts among skilled laborers arose in the attempt to preserve the "functional autonomy" of the craftsmen. Gutman (1976: 36-37) relates this point to the cooperage craftsmen in late nineteenth-century America. I shall demonstrate later that this also held in part for the coopers of Minneapolis.

7. Two years later (in the spring of 1870), upon hearing news that the journeymen's wages would be cut from 15 to 12.5 cents per barrel, Curtis arranged with three others to start another cooperative. This quickly failed because the treasurer, Lawrence Stoker pulled a *coup d'etat* on the others, as he personally managed to secure a lucrative contract with one of the mills and started a boss shop of his own (Shaw 1886: 13), and later employed cheap prison labor during the cooper strikes of 1879 (*Minneapolis Tribune*, July 18, 1879).

8. *Minneapolis Daily Tribune*, November 27 and 30, 1872. Relying upon coopers brought in from Milwaukee seems to have been commonplace during periods of strikes, and dates least as far back as 1866, when barrel makers were asking 25 cents a barrel in light of a firm offer of 20 cents per barrel (*St. Paul Daily Press*, August 28, 1866).

9. *Minneapolis Tribune*, August 26 and 27, 1874. It was not until 1878 that the

first local assembly of the Knights of Labor was organized in Minneapolis (Engberg 1941: 368).

10. *St. Paul Daily Dispatch*, December 3 and 4, 1874; *Minneapolis Tribune*, December 3, 1874. An interesting question for future research is how a newly formed cooperative was able to establish such a lucrative contract.

11. The bylaws are cited in full by Shaw (1886: 18-20) and Myrick (1895: 139-42).

12. Section 2 of the law which deals with the distribution of profits states that "no distribution shall be declared and paid until a sum equal, at least, to ten per cent. of the net profits shall be appropriated for a contingent or sinking fund, until there shall have accumulated a sum equal to thirty per cent. in excess of such capital stock." This was later dropped entirely in an 1881 amendment, largely due to the response of the cooperative coopers. See Shaw (1888: 311).

13. *Minneapolis Tribune*, November 20, 1877. Unfortunately the article does not say whether or not it was the cooperatives that remained in business.

14. For instance, the Anson cooper shops had men who could produce up to thirty barrels a day (*Minneapolis Tribune*, December 25, 1875), while Barttell and Company, which relied heavily on machinery, had the capacity to produce between 2,500 and 3,000 barrels per day (*Minneapolis Tribune*, May 29, 1876). Also see Shaw (1886: 23).

15. Further archival research may allow us to determine the extent to which any problems may have arisen between the journeymen who did not enjoy membership status and those coopers who had full membership rights.

16. Although the cooperatives and journeymen constituted the Cooper's Assembly of the Knights of Labor, I have found no evidence that the Knights funded or encouraged capital formation among the cooperative shops. Capital was, however, loaned by Minneapolis banks.

17. G. O. Virtue argued that "the displacement of a large amount of hand work involved in the use of these machines was resisted as long as possible by the cooperative companies, for they were composed of men whose chief interest lay in the employment of the skill they had acquired" (1905: 538).

18. As far back as October, 1872, complaints were raised in the *Coopers Monthly Journal* concerning a barrel factory in St. Louis:

The barrels were raised by boys, clamped and trussed by machinery, the heads were turned by machines and put into the barrels by boys, and there was nothing left for the coopers to do but plane, shave up and hoop the package. When a barrel was finished, it generally leaked at every joint. . . . But the staves were kiln dried and by the pouring from one to four pints of water in each barrel . . . it could be made to pass. All this was very well and as the company warranted every package they were not in want of a market. (quoted in Commons and Associates 1926: 74)

Perlman notes that "The effects of such a change in making barrels is obvious. The cooper was now deprived of the protection afforded by his skill. His part in the process now was trimming the barrel instead of making it" (Commons and Associates 1926: 75). Also, in his history of the cooperage industry in the United States, Coyne wrote:

the old hand cooper was entirely eliminated with the introduction of perfected cooperage machinery, and men could be quickly trained for the minor hand operations remaining in barrel manufacture. Many of the old hand coopers found employment in machine cooper shops, however, some [were] employed in repairing leaks and defects which developed in the testing operations, and others were merged with the workers who finished the barrel as it came from the crozer, and who were henceforth known by the lowly name of "hoopers" instead of "coopers," or sometimes designated as "hooper-coopers." (1940: 24)

19. Virtue noted that the Hennepin shop attempted to introduce a "heading up" machine, an invention of one of its members, only to have it later taken out, partly because of imperfections, but also because of a strong opposition among the membership (1905: 543-44). Examples such as this point to the importance of further detailed research.

20. In 1895 the cost of producing 100 flour barrels averaged $12.63 for hand labor, $3.85 for machine. It took 50.5 hours for the former, 22.33 hours for the latter (*Thirteenth Annual Report of the Commissioner of Labor. Hand and Machine Labor, Volume I* (1898), p. 41).

21. *Leonard's Twentieth Century Cooperage Directory and Telegraphic Code* (1899) lists the Hennepin County, Minneapolis Cooperage Co., and the North Star Barrel Co. as machine shops. The Cooperative Barrel Co. is not explicitly listed as a machine shop. The only shops selling flour barrels which were produced by hand were W. L. Dudrey (in Moorhead) and the Reichert Cooperage Company (in Red Wing), neither of which were in Minneapolis.

22. The burden of bag competition from New York and St. Louis dates at least as far back as 1879. See the *Stillwater Gazette* (February 19, 1879).

23. In 1901 the trade journal *Barrel and Box* tried to begin a counter movement against the Eastern trade. One drawing shows a flour barrel with the following inscription: "LET'S MAKE A TRUST to improve the slack cooperage industry. BUY FLOUR IN A BARREL, thereby increasing the market for barrels, staves, heading and hoops, and giving employment to more people in the industry. For information and stickers write THE BARREL AND BOX." During this time, the cooperage industry began sponsoring, apparently, the barrel stunts over Niagara Falls. For instance, on October 24, 1901, the West Bay Cooperage Company of Buffalo, New York made a barrel "constructed especially for [the] purpose" of Annie Edson Taylor to take a drop over the Falls. The account of the incident says "we are pleased with the ability of our coopers to make a barrel that will stand the racket," yet continues "still, the lady is old enough to have more gumption, and she ought to have been spanked and put to bed instead of taking such a foolish trip" (quoted in Coyne 1940: 36). Perhaps the point was that a barrel was much more reliable than a bag.

24. It is hard to pinpoint exactly when a given cooperative lost its truly cooperative format. Economists have different judgements. Watkins (1922: 555) recognized a tendency toward joint-stockism during the 1910s; in 1905 Virtue regarded the North Star as "nothing but a joint stock company of 40 members owning the stock in equal amounts" (1905: 541); Engberg (1941: 373) went so far to say that the competition with sacks and the introduction of machinery "resulted in lower wages, strikes, and, finally, failure for the cooperatives by 1887," though it is not at all clear in what respect he considered them failures.

CHAPTER 7 _____

Conclusion

MARXISM AND SELF-MANAGEMENT

In 1985 Mihailo Marković wrote:

> The alternative offered by Marx—a disalienated, emancipated human community without classes, repressive professional state, without any monopoly of dominating power, a community in which every individual acquires full possibility of participation in social decision-making and of self-development—remains the optimal historical possibility of our time, or if you like the most human utopian ideal of our time. (1985: 37)

But the knowledge problem posed by the Austrian school of economics, and the crushing weight of evidence exposed through the fall of 1989, suggest that the Marxist road to self-management must be rejected. Neither Marx himself nor his contemporary followers could overcome the tension between comprehensive planning and self-management, centralization and decentralization.

Marx's praxis philosophy is grounded in a concept of totality that, as Martin Jay recently demonstrated (1984), has lost its credibility and persuasiveness. Critics of the market system, from Marx to Marković, believed the concept of praxis supplies an Archimedean point for criticism: "In praxis and on the basis of praxis," wrote Karel Kosík, "man transcends the closed character of animality and of inorganic nature and constitutes his relationship with the world in its totality. In his openness, man as a finite being transcends his finitude and establishes contact with the totality of the world" (1976: 140). Marković claimed that "Marx's philosophy is the only one that deals with the problem of making history." To which he added: "The main point in Marx['s] critique of the entire civilization of our epoch is that man cannot bring to life the optimal possibility of his being—a rational, free, creative, social life in existing historical conditions" (1985: 41).

From the praxis benchmark, the market system apparently created a gap between human existence and human essence. Praxis allows critics to condemn the market system *in toto*, to demand the abolition, the *aufhebung*, of the spontaneous market process in favor of democratic, fully participatory planning.

In practice, however, revolutionary praxis has led to nothing short of chaos and disorder. We are not praxis beings in Marx's sense of the term. Part of what it means to be a human is to live within social institutions (most notably the market process) that have evolved as the unintended, undesigned outcomes of human action. To abolish the market system would be to destroy the *raison d'être* of advanced civilization. As Jürgen Habermas recently admitted:

Marxists . . . have to ask themselves whether socialism today, under present conditions, can still really mean a *total* democratic restructuration from top to bottom, and vice versa, of the economic system: that is, a transformation of the capitalist economy according to models of self-management and council-based administration. I myself do not believe so. (Dews 1986: 67; cf. pp. 45-46)

SELF-MANAGEMENT AND MARKET PROCESSES: THOUGHTS ABOUT THE FUTURE

This does not imply that cooperative and self-managed enterprises must be forsaken for the market economy. Viewed from a comparative systems perspective, the spontaneous market process allows property owners to adjust to relative scarcities and coordinate a bewildering array of production and consumption plans. The virtue of the general principles of private property and unhampered market exchange is that it allows individuals to decide upon the specific organizational forms or uses of that property. It allows both corporate managers and worker-owners to use their entrepreneurial faculties to adjust to the changing demands of the community.

The virtue of the workers' cooperative in particular rests partly, I believe, in its emphasis on dialogue. Now I have argued that the advocates of a workers' self-managed socialist system have misunderstood the nature of dialogue. Society cannot rely upon dialogue "alone," that is, dialogical planning without unhampered markets to achieve a rationally coordinated system. And the Austrian economists have realized this for quite some time now. But while the Austrians understand that the system as a whole cannot be scientifically manipulated in a rational manner, they have perhaps (through their relative silence) misunderstood the degree to which a business enterprise can.

Certainly a business organization is the product of human design and based upon an *ex ante* plan. But the idea that humans can be treated and manipulated like mere inputs has become discredited over the past few decades. The scientific management movement, for example, has proven futile. Indeed, as we move toward the twenty first century one hears more about "chaos" in management circles compared to "scientific control." Perhaps here a greater emphasis will be placed on conventional dialogue between workers and their superiors. After all, the plant manager and shop floor worker do not communicate their day to day production activities to one another through market price signals. A worker may be able to articulate quite a bit of contextual knowledge through genuine dialogue with others in the firm and perhaps this could increase a firm's overall efficiency or profitability. Here democratic participation as opposed to technical, scientific control alone may prove useful, and, consequently, the dialogical basis of the cooperative form may be seen in a new light. Neither the face-to-face dialogue of the firm nor the distant "dialogue" and discovery procedure of the market should be dispensed with.

The cooperative organizational format provides workers with a greater voice in the firm's overall production plan (this in addition to the "exit" option of the traditional firm). Hence, workers not only express their preferences indirectly through labor markets, but directly in the workshop as well. The ability to choose between "voice" and "exit," instead of being forced to submit to one or the other, should be an improvement from the worker's point of view. The right to participate also helps break down the impersonal nature of standard business hierarchies. It provides a better opportunity for those who wish to foster a sense of community in the workplace rather than what may feel like blind obedience to bureaucratic authority.

When workers are free to establish their own cooperative organizations and plan production processes according to their own judgement, work may become more meaningful in itself. Indeed, workers may become more aware of the truly social nature of producing as a team of co-owners, as they join together to create, structure, and carry out a common goal, instead of simply working for a wage to satisfy ends predominantly outside the workplace.

The advantages of dialogue, participatory democracy, and a greater sense of community offset to some degree the disadvantages of monitoring and principal-agent problems in the cooperative firm.[1]

Will the cooperative form become dominant? Probably not. But there

are reasons to believe that it will continue to grow as we turn from the
rationalist spirit of modernity toward a more "post-industrial" world. Because the market system, as it exists in the West, for example, does not
(contrary to the claims of some of its supporters) represent the best of all
possible worlds, it is quite probable that current forms of business organization will evolve over time. One should expect that to happen in an
unhampered market system, for our knowledge of business organization
must inevitably change. And so must the knowledge of workers. We are
quickly discovering that workers embody an inalienable intellectual component. Today both Taylorism and Marxism are on the run. Workers are
now learning details of skilled behavior, which make it all the more difficult
for a boss to dispose of a worker without losing the greater part of his
investment.[2]

The question of the future viability of workers' self-managed firms is at
once a question of meaningful theory and relevant practice. Market advocates should reconsider the extent to which existing property rights improve as well as hold back technological and organizational progress. What
F. A. Hayek stated in the midst of the socialist calculation debate (1935)
is still relevant today: "There is no reason to assume that the historically
given legal institutions are necessarily the most 'natural' in any sense. The
recognition of the principle of private property does not by any means
necessarily imply that the particular delimitation of the contents of this
right as determined by the existing laws are the most appropriate" (1975:
22). Given the issues raised in this book, I am inclined to believe that a
freeing up of the market system could further encourage the development
of self-managed enterprise.

NOTES

1. It is worth mentioning that not all neoclassical economists agree on the extent
to which the disincentives problems posed by Alchian and Demsetz (1972) and
others such as Holmstrom (1982) militate against the cooperative format. For
example, Oliver Williamson (1975) has argued that excessive monitoring may actually lower the performance and morale of team workers. All too often, however,
the unintended, undesirable consequences of monitoring such as this are overlooked
in the theoretical literature (cf. Putterman 1984: 176-77). Moreover, when one
considers the degree to which our knowledge is embodied in tacit skills and judgement (cf. Polanyi 1958; Lavoie 1986c), the extent to which real world monitors
can technically obtain the information required for efficient metering as the models
suggest becomes somewhat questionable. Williamson's awareness of information
being "impacted" within a team of workers accords well with this view of knowledge: much of the knowledge embodied in team production may not be adequately
observed by a monitor or efficiently communicated to a central metering authority.
In fact, each team worker may have a better idea of what the others are doing
(and are able to do) than a monitor, even though any particular worker may not

be able to articulate that knowledge to a monitor. Under these cases the cooperative format may handle the monitoring problem more effectively than the traditional business organization.

Alchian and Demsetz recognize this type of knowledge among "artistic" and "professional" work (1972: 92-93) and thereby admit that boss-type monitoring in these cases may not be effective or desirable. If the Polanyi-Lavoie position holds—that inarticulate knowledge is the basis of human action—then the extent to which most work has an "artistic" element becomes all the more likely and the effectiveness of boss-type monitoring in most cases is open to debate.

2. Consider, for example, the recent wave of "break-away" firms in the computer industry. Old firms act as embryos for new firms. If a worker or group of workers is not satisfied with the existing firm, each has a skill which he or she controls, and can leave the firm with those skills and establish a new one. In the information age it is becoming more evident that a boss cannot control the workers as one did in the days when the assembly line was dominant. People cannot be treated as workhorses any longer, for the value of the production process is becoming increasingly embodied in the intellectual skills of the worker. This poses a new threat to the traditional firm if it denies participatory organization.

The appearance of break-away computer firms leads one to question the extent to which our existing system of property rights in ideas and information actually protects bosses in other industries against the countervailing power of workers. Perhaps our current system of patents, copyrights, and other intellectual property rights not only impedes competition and fosters monopoly, as some Austrians argue. Intellectual property rights may also reduce the likelihood of break-away firms in general, and discourage the shift to more participatory, cooperative formats.

Bibliography

Albert, Michael, and Robin Hahnel. 1978. *Unorthodox Marxism: An Essay on Capitalism, Socialism, and Revolution*. Boston: South End Press.

Alchian, Armen A., and Harold Demsetz. 1972. "Production, Information Costs, and Economic Theory," *American Economic Review* 62, no. 5 (December). Reprinted in Armen A. Alchian, *Economic Forces at Work* (Indianapolis: Liberty Press, 1977), pp. 73-110.

Arrow, Kenneth J., and F. H. Hahn. 1971. *General Competitive Analysis*. San Francisco: Holden-Day.

Avineri, Shlomo. 1968. *The Social and Political Thought of Karl Marx*. New York: Cambridge University Press.

Babić, Mate. 1980. "Some Aspects of Plan Coordination in Yugoslavia," *Economic Analysis and Workers' Management* 4, no. 14.

Bajt, A. 1968a. "Property in Capital and in the Means of Production in Socialist Economies," *Journal of Law and Economics* 11 (April).

———. 1968b. "Social Ownership—Collective and Individual," in Horvat, Marković, and Supek (1975, vol. 2), pp. 151-63.

Bakunin, Michael. 1873. *Statism and Anarchy*. In Bakunin (1971), pp. 323-53.

———. 1866. *Revolutionary Catechism*. In Bakunin (1971), pp. 76-97.

———. 1970. *God and the State*. New York: Dover.

———. 1971. *Bakunin on Anarchy* (Sam Dolgoff, ed.). New York: Vintage Books.

Barnard, Charles. 1881. *Cooperation as a Business*. New York: G. P. Putnam's Sons.

Barns, William E. (ed.). 1971. *The Labor Problem*. New York: Arno Press.

Barone, Enrico. 1908. "The Ministry of Production in the Collectivist State," in Hayek (1975), pp. 245-90.

Baumgartner, Tom, Tom R. Burns, and Duško Sekulić. 1979. "Self-Management, Market, and Political Institutions in Conflict: Yugoslav Development Patterns and Dialectics," in Tom R. Burns, Lars Karlsson, and Veljko Rus (eds.), *Work and Power: The Liberation of Work and the Control of Political Power* (Beverly Hills, Calif.: Sage Publications, Inc., 1979), pp. 81-138.

Beard, Mary Ritter. 1969. *The American Labor Movement*. New York: Arno Press.

Beecher, Jonathan, and Richard Bienvenu (eds.). 1983. *The Utopian Vision of Charles Fourier* (trans. by Beecher and Bienvenu). Columbia: University of Missouri Press.

Bell, Daniel, and Irving Kristol (eds.). 1981. *The Crisis in Economic Theory*. New York: Basic Books.

Ben-Ner, Avner. 1984. "On the Stability of the Cooperative Type of Organization," *Journal of Comparative Economics* 8.

Ben-Ner, Avner, and Egon Neuberger. 1979. "On the Economics of Self-Management: The Israeli Kibbutz and the Yugoslav Enterprise," *Economic Analysis and Workers' Management* 13, no. 1-2.

Bernstein, Richard J. 1983. *Beyond Objectivism and Relativism: Science, Hermeneutics, and Praxis*. Philadelphia: University of Pennsylvania Press.

Bičanić, Ivo. 1989. "The Scope for Self-Management in the Yugoslav Enterprise," paper delivered at the conference "Self-Management in Future Socialism and Capitalism," (Dubrovnik: Inter-University Center of postgraduate studies, March 6-17, 1989).

Bislev, Claus. 1985. "Planning in a Worker-Managed Economy," *Economic Analysis and Workers' Management* 24, no. 4.

Boettke, Peter J. 1990a. "Interpretive Reasoning and the Study of Social Life, *Methodus* 2, no. 2 (December).

———. 1990b. *The Political Economy of Soviet Socialism: The Formative Years, 1918–1928*. Boston: Kluwer Academic.

Bonin, John P. 1977. "Work Incentives and Uncertainty on a Collective Farm," *Journal of Comparative Economics*. 1.

———. 1980. "On the Theory of the Competitive Labor-Managed Firm under Price Uncertainty: A Correction," *Journal of Comparative Economics* 4, no. 3 (September).

———. 1984. "Membership and Employment in an Egalitarian Cooperative," *Economica* 51, no. 203 (August).

Bonin, John P., and Louis Putterman. 1987. *Economics of Cooperation and the Labor-Managed Economy*. New York: Harwood Academic Publishers.

Bottomore, Tom (ed.). 1988. *Interpretations of Marx*. New York: Basil Blackwell.

———. 1990. *The Socialist Economy: Theory and Practice*. New York: Guilford Press.

Bottomore, Tom, et al. (eds). 1983. *A Dictionary of Marxist Thought*. Cambridge, Mass.: Harvard University Press.

Bradley, Keith, and Alan Gelb. 1981. "Motivation and Control in the Mondragon Experiment," *British Journal of Industrial Relations* 19.

Brewer, A. A., and M. J. Browning. 1982. "On the 'Employment' Decision of a Labour-Managed Firm," *Economica* 49, no. 194 (May).

Brutzkus, Boris. 1935. *Economic Planning in Soviet Russia*. London: Routledge and Sons.

Buber, Martin. 1958. *Paths in Utopia*. Boston: Beacon Press.

Buchanan, James. 1969. *Cost and Choice*. Chicago: University of Chicago Press.

Bukharin, Nikolai, and E. Preobrazhensky. 1966. *The ABC of Communism*. Ann Arbor: University of Michigan Press.

Caldwell, Bruce. 1982. *Beyond Positivism: Economic Methodology in the Twentieth Century*. Boston: George Allen and Unwin.

Carpenter, Kenneth E. (ed.). 1972. *Cooperative Communities: Plans and Descriptions, Eleven Pamphlets, 1825–1847*. New York: Arno Press.

Carter, April. 1982. *Democratic Reform in Yugoslavia: The Changing Role of the Party*. London: Frances Printer.

Catlin, Warren B. 1926. *The Labor Problem*. New York: Harper and Brothers.

Clark, Fred J. 1904. "Flour Barrels in Minneapolis in the Northwest," *National Cooper's Journal*. (May).

Clark, John Bates. 1967. *The Philosophy of Wealth*. New York: Augustus M. Kelley.

Clark, John Maurice. 1967. *Preface to Social Economics: Essays on Economic Theory and Social Problems*. New York: Augustus M. Kelley.

Colander, David, and Arjo Klamer. 1987. "The Making of an Economist," *Journal of Economic Perspectives* 3, no. 2 (Fall).

Cole, G. D. H. 1971. *Economic Planning*. Port Washington, N.Y.: Kennikat Press.

Comisso, Ellen Turkish. 1979. *Workers' Control under Plan and Market: Implications of Yugoslav Self-Management*. New Haven: Yale University Press.

Commons, John R. 1911. "Unions and Efficiency," *American Economic Review* (September). Reprinted in Commons (1964), pp. 135-48.

———. 1964. *Labor and Administration*. New York: Augustus M. Kelley.

Commons, John R., and Associates. 1926. *History of Labour in the United States* vol. 2. New York: Macmillan.

The Constitution of the Socialist Federal Republic of Yugoslavia Belgrade 1974. Ljubljana: Dopisna Delavska Univerza, n.d.

Conte, Michael A. 1979. "Short Run Dynamics of the Labour-Managed Firm," *Economic Analysis and Workers' Management* 13, no. 1-2.

———. 1980. "On the Economic Theory of the Labor-Managed Firm in the Short Run," *Journal of Comparative Economics* 4, no. 2 (June).

Cowen, Tyler, and Richard Fink. 1985. "Inconsistent Equilibrium Constructs: The ERE of Mises and Rothbard," *American Economic Review* 75, no. 4 (September).

Coyne, Franklin E. 1940. *The Development of the Cooperage Industry in the United States, 1620-1940*. Chicago: Lumber Buyer's Publishing Co.

Dallmayr, Fred R., and Thomas A. McCarthy (eds.). 1977. *Understanding and Social Inquiry*. Notre Dame: University of Notre Dame Press.

Dews, Peter (ed.). 1986. *Autonomy and Solidarity: Interviews with Jurgen Habermas*. London: Verso.

Djilas, Milovan. 1990. "Eastern Europe: The Revolution and its Future," *Global Affairs* (Spring).

Dolan, Edwin (ed.). 1976. *The Foundations of Modern Austrian Economics*. Kansas City: Sheed and Ward, Inc.

Domar, Evsey D. 1966. "The Soviet Collective Farm as a Producer Cooperative," *American Economic Review* 56, no. 4, part 1 (September).

Dorfman, Joseph. 1969. *The Economic Mind in American Civilization, 1865-1918* (vol. 3). New York: Augustus M. Kelley.

Dreze, Jacques H. 1976. "Some Theory of Labor Management and Participation," *Econometrica*, 44, no. 6 (November).

Ebeling, Richard M. 1986. "Toward a Hermeneutical Economics," in Kirzner (1986), pp. 39-55.

———. 1987. "Cooperation in Anonymity," *Critical Review* 1, no. 4 (Fall).

Edwards, Stewart (ed.). 1973. *The Communards of Paris, 1871*. Ithaca, N.Y.: Cornell University Press.

Ely, Richard T. 1886. "Co-operation in Literature and the State," in Barns (1971), pp. 6-16.

———. 1887. "Co-operation," *Chautaquan* 8, no. 3 (December).

———. 1969. *The Labor Movement in America*. New York: Arno Press.

———. 1971. *Studies in the Evolution of Industrial Society* 2 vols. Port Washington, N.Y.: Kennikat Press.

Engberg, George B. 1941. "The Knights of Labor in Minnesota," *Minnesota History* vol. 22. Saint Paul: Minnesota Historical Society.

Engels, Frederick. 1978. *Anti-Dühring*. Moscow: Progress Publishers.

Estrin, Saul. 1985. "Self-Managed and Capitalist Behavior in Alternative Market Structures," *Advances in the Economic Analysis of Participatory and Labor-Managed Firms* vol. 1.

Fama, Eugene. 1970. "Efficient Capital Markets: A Review of Theory and Empirical Work," *Journal of Finance* (May).

Fawcett, Henry. 1872. *Essays and Lectures*. London: Macmillan and Co.

———. 1888. *Manual of Political Economy* (7th ed.). New York: Macmillan and Co.

Fayol, Henri. 1949. *General and Industrial Management*. London: Pitman Publishing Co.

Fetter, Frank A. 1922. *Modern Economic Problems* vol. 2 (2nd ed., revised). New York: The Century Co.

Fink, Richard. 1991. *Price Theory and Pricing Practices*. New York: Basil Blackwell.

Fourier, Charles. 1828. *De l'anarchie industrielle et scientific*, partly reprinted in Beecher and Bienvenu (1983), pp. 122-28.

———. 1971. *Design for Utopia: Selected Writings of Charles Fourier*. New York: Schocken Books.

Friedman, Milton. 1962. *Capitalism and Freedom*. Chicago: University of Chicago Press.

Fromm, Erich (ed.). 1965. *Socialist Humanism: An International Symposium*. Garden City, N.J.: Doubleday and Co.

Furubotn, E. 1971. "Toward a Dynamic Model of the Yugoslav Firm," *Canadian Journal of Economics* 4 (May).

Furubotn, Eirik G., and Svetozar Pejovich. 1970. "Property Rights and the Behavior of the Firm in a Socialist State: The Example of Yugoslavia," *Zeitschrift für Nationaloekonomie* vol. 30.

———. 1972. "Property Rights and Economic Theory: A Survey of the Recent Literature," *Journal of Economic Literature* 10, no. 4 (December).

———— (eds.). 1974a. *The Economics of Property Rights*. Cambridge, Mass.: Bal-
    linger.

————. 1974b. "The Importance of Incentives," in Furubotn and Pejovich (eds.)
    (1974a), pp. 169-72.

Gadamer, Hans-Georg. 1985. *Truth and Method*. New York: Crossroad.

Gal-Or, Esther, Michael Landsberger, and Abraham Subotnik. 1980. "Allocation
    and Distributional Effects of a Monopolistically Competitive Firm in a Co-
    operative Economy," *Journal of Comparative Economics* 4, no. 2 (June).

Garlock, Jonathan. 1982. *Guide to the Local Assemblies of the Knights of Labor*.
    Westport, Conn.: Greenwood Press.

Golubović, Zagorka. 1981. "Stalinism and Socialism," *Praxis International* vol. 1,
    no. 2 (July).

————. 1985. "Where We Are At—When Marxism is Concerned?", in Gajo Pe-
    trović and Wolfdietrich Schmied-Kowarzich (1985), pp. 169-78.

Gorz, André. 1989. *Critique of Economic Reason*. New York: Verso.

Grassl, Wolfgang, and Barry Smith (eds.). 1986. *Austrian Economics: Historical
    and Philosophical Background*. New York: New York University Press.

Gregory, Paul R., and Robert C. Stuart. 1981. *Soviet Economic Structure and
    Performance*. New York: Harper and Row.

Grossman, Gregory. 1963. "Notes for a Theory of the Command Economy," *Soviet
    Studies* 15, no. 2 (October).

Guerin, Daniel. 1970. *Anarchism: From Theory to Practice*. New York: Monthly
    Review Press.

Gunn, Christopher Eaton. 1984. *Workers' Self-Management in the United States*.
    Ithaca: Cornell University Press.

Gutman, Herbert G. 1976. *Work, Culture, and Society in Industrializing America:
    Essays in Working Class and Social History*. New York: Alfred A. Knopf.

Haan, Norma, Robert N. Bellah, Paul Rabinow, and William M. Sullivan (eds.).
    1983. *Social Science as Moral Inquiry*. New York: Cambridge University
    Press.

Habermas, Jürgen. 1970. *Toward a Rational Society: Student Protest, Science and
    Politics*. Boston: Beacon Press.

————. 1975. *Legitimation Crisis*. Boston: Beacon Press.

Hadley, Arthur Twining. 1896. *Economics: An Account of the Relations Between
    Private Property and Social Welfare*. New York: G. P. Putnam's Sons.

Hahn, Frank. 1973. *On the Notion of Equilibrium in Economics*. Cambridge:
    Cambridge University Press.

————. 1981. "General Equilibrium Theory," in Bell and Kristol (1981), pp. 123-
    38.

Hay, John D., and John Suckling. 1980. "On the Theory of the Competitive Labor-
    Managed Firm under Price Uncertainty: Comment," *Journal of Comparative
    Economics* 4, no. 3 (September).

Hayek, F. A. 1937. "Economics and Knowledge," *Economica*. Vol. 4, n.s. Re-
    printed in Hayek (1948), pp. 33-56.

————. 1940. "Socialist Calculation III: The Competitive 'Solution' " from *Econ-
    omica* 7, no. 26 (n.s.). Reprinted in Hayek (1948), pp. 181-208.

————. 1944. *The Road to Serfdom*. Chicago: University of Chicago Press.

————. 1945. "The Use of Knowledge in Society," *American Economic Review*. Reprinted in Hayek (1948), pp. 77-91.

————. 1948. *Individualism and Economic Order*. Chicago: University of Chicago Press.

————. 1968. "Competition as a Discovery Procedure," *Kieler Vortage* n.s. 56. Reprinted in Hayek (1978), pp. 179-90.

———— (ed.). 1975. *Collectivist Economic Planning: Critical Studies on the Possibilities of Socialism*. Clifton, N.J.: Augustus M. Kelley.

————. 1978. *New Studies in Philosophy, Politics Economics and the History of Ideas*. Chicago: University of Chicago Press.

————. 1988. *The Fatal Conceit: The Errors of Socialism*. Chicago: University of Chicago Press.

Hekman, Susan J. 1986. *Hermeneutics and the Sociology of Knowledge*. Notre Dame: University of Notre Dame Press.

Heilbroner, Robert L. 1967. *The Worldly Philosophers* 3rd ed. New York: Simon and Schuster.

Heller, Agnes. "Labour and Human Needs in a Society of Associated Producers." In Bottomore (1988), pp. 190-200.

High, Jack. 1990. *Maximizing, Action, and Market Adjustment: An Inquiry into the Theory of Economic Disequilibrium*. Munich: Philosophia Verlag.

Hill, Martin, and Michael Waterson. 1983. "Labor-Managed Cournot Oligipoly and Industry Output," *Journal of Comparative Economics* 7, no. 1 (March).

Hoff, T. J. B. 1949. *Economic Calculation in the Socialist Society*. London: William Hodge and Co., Ltd.

Hofstadter, Richard. 1945. *Social Darwinism in American Thought, 1860-1915*. Philadelphia: University of Pennsylvania Press.

Hollinger, Robert (ed.). 1985. *Hermeneutics and Praxis*. Notre Dame: University of Notre Dame Press.

Holmstrom, B. 1979. "Moral Hazard and Observability," *Bell Journal of Economics* 10, no. 1 (Spring).

————. 1982. "Moral Hazard in Teams," *Bell Journal of Economics* 13, no. 2 (Autumn).

Horvat, Branko. 1964. "The Pricing of Factors of Production," from *Towards a Theory of Planned Economy* (Belgrade: Yugoslav Institute of Economic Research). Reprinted in Horvat, Marković, and Supek (1975), vol. 2, pp. 294-306.

————. 1967. "Prilog zasnivanju teorije jugoslavenskog produzeca," *Ekonomska Analiza* 1, no. 1-2.

————. 1972. "An Institutional Model of a Self-managed Socialist Economy," *Eastern European Economics*. Vol. 10, no. 4 (Summer). Reprinted in Horvat, Marković, and Supek (1975), vol. 2, pp. 307-27.

————. 1975a. "A New Social System in the Making: Historical Origins and Development of Self-governing Socialism." In Horvat, Marković, and Supek (1975), vol. 1, pp. 3-66.

————. 1975b. "On the Theory of the Labor-managed Firm." In Horvat, Marković, and Supek (1975), vol. 2, pp. 229-40.

————. 1976. *The Yugoslav Economic System: The First Labor-Managed Economy in the Making*. White Plains, N.Y.: International Arts and Sciences Press.

————. 1980. "Searching for a Strategy of Transition," *Economic Analysis and Workers' Management* 14, no. 3.

————. 1982. *The Political Economy of Socialism: A Marxist Social Theory*. Armonk, N.Y.: M. E. Sharpe, Inc.

————. 1986. "Farewell to the Illyrian Firm," *Economic Analysis and Workers' Management* 20, no. 1.

Horvat, Branko, Mihailo Marković, and Rudi Supek (eds.). 1975. *Self-Governing Socialism: A Reader*. Two volumes. White Plains, N.Y.: International Arts and Sciences Press.

Ichiishi, Tatsuro. 1977. "Coalition Structure in a Labor-Managed Market Economy," *Econometrica* 45, no. 2 (March).

Inselbaq, Isik, and Murat Sertel. 1979. "The Workers' Enterprise under Uncertainty in a Mixed Economy," *Economic Analysis and Workers' Management* 13, no. 1-2.

Ireland, Norman J., and Peter J. Law. 1978. "An Enterprise Incentive Fund for Labor Mobility in the Cooperative Economy," *Economica* 45, no. 178 (May).

————. 1981. "Efficiency, Incentives, and Individual Labor Supply in the Labor-Managed Firm," *Journal of Comparative Economics* 5, no. 1 (March).

————. 1982. *The Economics of Labor-Managed Enterprise*. New York: St. Martin's Press.

Israelsen, Dwight L. 1980. "Collectives, Communes, and Incentives," *Journal of Comparative Economics* 4, no. 2 (June).

Jaffe, W. 1976. "Menger, Jevons and Walras De-homogenized," *Economic Inquiry* 14.

Jay, Martin. 1984. *Marxism and Totality: The Adventures of a Concept from Lukacs to Habermas*. Berkeley: University of California Press.

Jay, Peter. 1980. "The Workers' Co-operative Economy," in Alasdair Clayre (ed.), *The Political Economy of Co-Operation and Participation: A Third Sector* (New York: Oxford University Press), pp. 9-45.

Jelley, S. M. 1969. *The Voice of Labor*. New York: Arno and the New York Times.

Jensen, Michael C., and William H. Meckling. 1979. "Rights and Production Functions: An Application to Labor-Managed Firms and Codetermination," *Journal of Business* 52 (October).

Jensen, Michael C., and Richard S. Ruback. 1983. "The Market for Corporate Control: The Scientific Evidence," *Journal of Financial Economics* 11 (April).

Jones, Derek C. 1977. "The Economics and Industrial Relations of Producer Cooperatives in the United States, 1791-1939," *Ekonomska Analiza* 11, no. 3-4.

————. 1979. "US Producer Cooperatives: The Record to Date," *Industrial Relations* 18, no. 3 (Fall).

————. 1980. "Producer Co-operatives in Industrialized Western Economies," *British Journal of Industrial Relations* 18 (July).

————. 1982. "The United States of America: A Survey of Producer Co-operative Performance." In Frank H. Stephen (ed.), *The Performance of Labour-Managed Firms* (New York: St. Martin's Press).

Kirzner, Israel M. 1973. *Competition and Entrepreneurship*. Chicago: University of Chicago Press.

———. 1978. *The Perils of Regulation: A Market-Process Approach*. Law and Economics Center Occasional Paper. Coral Gables, Fla.: University of Miami Law School.

———. 1979. *Perception, Opportunity, and Profit: Studies in the Theory of Entrepreneurship*. Chicago: University of Chicago Press.

——— (ed.). 1982. *Method, Process, and Austrian Economics: Essays in Honor of Ludwig von Mises*. Lexington, Mass.: Lexington Books.

———. 1984. "Economic Planning and the Knowledge Problem," *Cato Journal* 4, no. 2 (Fall).

———. 1985. *Discovery and the Capitalist Process*. Chicago: University of Chicago Press.

——— (ed.). 1986. *Subjectivism, Intelligibility, and Economic Understanding: Essays in Honor of Ludwig M. Lachmann on his Eightieth Birthday*. New York: New York University Press.

Knapp, Joseph G. 1969. *The Rise of American Cooperative Enterprise: 1620-1920*. Danville, Ill.: The Interstate Printers and Publishers, Inc.

Knapp, Joseph G., and Associates. 1967. *Great American Cooperators: Bibliographical Sketches of 101 Major Pioneers in Cooperative Development*. Washington, DC: American Institute of Cooperation.

Knight, Frank H. 1971. *Risk, Uncertainty, and Profit*. Chicago: University of Chicago Press.

Kolko, Gabriel. 1963. *The Triumph of Conservatism*. Chicago: Quadrangle Books.

Kosík, Karel. 1976. *Dialectics of the Concrete: A Study on Problems of Man and World*. Boston: D. Reidel

Krešić, Andrija. 1968. "Political Dictatorship: The Conflict of Politics and Society," in Marković and Petrović (1979), pp. 121-37.

Kuhn, Thomas S. 1970. *The Structure of Scientific Revolutions*. 2nd edition. Chicago: University of Chicago Press.

Lachmann, Ludwig M. 1971. *The Legacy of Max Weber*. Berkeley: Glendessary Press.

———. 1977. *Capital, Expectations, and the Market Process: Essays in the Theory of the Market Economy* (edited and introduced by Walter Grinder). Kansas City: Sheed Andrews and McMeel, Inc.

———. 1978. *Capital and its Structure*. Kansas City: Sheed Andrews and McMeel, Inc.

———. 1986. *The Market as an Economic Process*. London: Basil Blackwell.

Laidler, Harry W. 1927. *A History of Socialist Thought*. New York: Thomas Y. Crowell Co.

Landsberger, Michael, and Abraham Subotnik. 1980. "Efficient Regulation of a Labor-Managed Monopolistic Firm," *European Economic Review* 13, no. 2 (March).

Lange, Oskar. 1936. "On the Economic Theory of Socialism." In Lippincott (ed.) (1964), pp. 57-143.

Lavoie, Don. 1981. "A Critique of the Standard Account of the Debate," *Journal of Libertarian Studies* 5, no. 1 (Winter).

————. 1985a. *National Economic Planning: What is Left?* Cambridge, Mass.: Ballinger Publishing Co.

————. 1985b. "The Interpretive Dimension of Economics: Science, Hermeneutics, and Praxeology," Center for the Study of Market Processes Working Paper no. 15. George Mason University.

————. 1985c. *Rivalry and Central Planning: The Socialist Calculation Debate Reconsidered.* New York: Cambridge University Press.

————. 1986a. "Between Institutionalism and Formalism: The Rise and Fall of the Austrian School's Calculation Argument, 1920-1950," paper presented at the Liberty Fund symposium on "The Problems of Economic Calculation under Socialism," January 25-27, 1986, New York University.

————. 1986b. "Euclideanism versus Hermeneutics: A Reinterpretation of Misesian Apriorism," in Kirzner (1986), pp. 192-210.

————. 1986c. "The Market as a Procedure for Discovery and Conveyance of Inarticulate Knowledge," *Comparative Economic Studies* 28, no. 1 (Spring).

————. 1986-1987. "Political and Economic Illusions of Socialism," *Critical Review* 1, no. 1 (Winter).

———— (ed.). 1991. *Hermeneutics and Economics.* New York: Routledge.

————. Forthcoming. *The Interpretive Turn: Essays in Continental Philosophy and Economics.*

Lenin, V. I. 1914. "The Taylor System-Man's Enslavement By the Machine," in V. I. Lenin, *On Workers' Control and the Nationalization of Industry* (Moscow: Progress Publishers, 1970), pp. 15-17.

————. 1943. *The State and Revolution.* New York: International Publishers.

Lerner, Abba. 1934. "Economic Theory and Socialist Economy," *Review of Economic Studies* 2.

————. 1944. *The Economics of Control: Principles of Welfare Economics.* New York: Macmillan.

Lippincott, Benjamin E. (ed.). 1964. *On the Economic Theory of Socialism.* New York: McGraw-Hill.

Littlechild, Stephen (ed.). 1990. *Austrian Economics* 3 vols. Brookfield, Vt.: Edward Elgar.

Lockwood, George B. 1905. *The New Harmony Movement.* NewYork: D. Appleton and Co.

Lydall, Harold. 1986. *Yugoslav Socialism: Theory and Practice.* New York: Oxford University Press.

McCloskey, Donald. 1985. *The Rhetoric of Economics.* Madison: University of Wisconsin Press.

Madison, G. B. 1989. "Hayek and the Interpretive Turn," *Critical Review* 3, no. 2 (Spring).

Malcomson, James M. 1984. "Work Incentives, Hierarchy, and Labour Markets," *Journal of Political Economy* 92, no. 3 (June).

Manne, Henry G. 1965. "Mergers and the Market for Corporate Control," *Journal of Political Economy* 73, no. 2 (April).

Marković, Mihailo. 1964. "Socialism and Self-management," *Praxis.* no. 2-3. Reprinted in Horvat, Marković, and Supek (1975) vol. 1, pp. 416-37.

————. 1974. *From Affluence to Praxis: Philosophy and Social Criticism.* Ann Arbor: University of Michigan Press.

————. 1975a. "Philosophical Foundations of the Idea of Self-management." In Horvat, Marković, and Supek (1975) vol. 1, pp. 327-50.

————. 1975b. "Self-government and Planning." In Horvat, Marković, and Supek (1975) vol. 1, pp. 479-90.

————. 1982. *Democratic Socialism: Theory and Practice*. New York: St. Martin's Press.

————. 1985. "Present-day Meaning of Marx's Theory." In Petrović and Schmied-Kowarzich (1985), pp. 35-41.

————. 1986. "Self-Governing Political System and De-alienation in Yugoslavia (1950-1965)," *Praxis International* 6, no. 2 (July).

Marković, Mihailo, and Gajo Petrović (eds.). 1979. *Praxis: Yugoslav Essays in the Philosophy and Methodology of the Social Sciences*. Boston: D. Reidel.

Marshall, Alfred. 1889. "Cooperation." In A.C. Pigou (ed.), *Memorials of Alfred Marshall* (New York: Augustus M. Kelley, 1966) pp. 227-55.

Marx, Karl. 1906. *Capital* (vol. 1). Chicago: Charles Kerr and Co.

————. 1909. *Capital* (vols. 2 and 3). Chicago: Charles Kerr and Co.

————. 1964. *The Economic and Philosophical Manuscripts of 1844*. New York: International Publishers.

————. 1970. *Critique of Hegel's 'Philosophy of Right'* (edited and introduced by Joseph O'Malley). New York: Cambridge University Press.

————. 1978. *The Poverty of Philosophy*. Moscow: Progress Publishers.

Marx, Karl, and Frederick Engels. 1969. *Selected Works* (vols. 1 and 2). Moscow: Progress Publishers.

————. 1970. *Selected Works* (vol. 3). Moscow: Progress Publishers.

Maurice, S. Charles, and C. E. Ferguson. 1976. "Factor Usage by a Labour-Managed Firm in a Socialist Economy," *Economica* n.s. 39, no. 153 (February).

Meade, James E. 1972. "The Theory of Labour-Managed Firms and Profit Sharing," *Economic Journal*. Reprinted in Vanek (ed.) (1975), pp. 394-421.

————. 1974. "Labour-Managed Firms in Conditions of Imperfect Competition," *Economic Journal* 84 (December).

————. 1979. "The Adjustment Processes of labour- Co-operatives with Constant Returns to Scale and Perfect Competition," *Economic Journal* 89, no. 356 (December).

Merkle, J. A. 1980. *Management and Ideology: The Legacy of the International Scientific Management Movement*. Berkeley: University of California Press.

Milenkovitch, Deborah D. 1971. *Plan and Market in Yugoslav Economic Thought*. New Haven: Yale University Press.

Mill, John Stuart. 1926. *Principles of Political Economy*. New York: Longmans, Green and Co., Ltd.

Millis, Harry A., and Royal E. Montgomery. 1945. *Organized Labor*. New York: McGraw-Hill.

Mirrlees, James A. 1976. "The Optimal Structure of Incentives and Authority Within an Organization," *Bell Journal of Economics* 7.

Mises, Ludwig von. 1920. "Economic Calculation in the Socialist Commonwealth." In Hayek (ed.) (1975), pp. 87-130.

————. 1962. *Liberalism: A Socio-Economic Exposition*. Kansas City: Sheed Andrews and McMeel.

———. 1966. *Human Action: A Treatise on Economics*. Chicago: Contemporary Books, Inc.

———. 1981a. *Epistemological Problems of Economics*. New York: New York University Press.

———. 1981b. *Socialism: An Economic and Sociological Analysis*. Indianapolis: Liberty Classics.

Miyazaki, Hajime, and Hugh M. Neary. 1983. "The Illyrian Firm Revisited," *Bell Journal of Economics* 14.

Monroe, Paul. 1896. "Profit Sharing in the United States," *American Journal of Sociology* 1 (May).

Montgomery, David. 1979. *Workers' Control in America*. New York: Cambridge University Press.

Montias, J. M. 1959. "Planning with Material Balances in Soviet-Type Economies," *American Economic Review* 49, no. 5 (December).

Mueller-Vollmer, Kurt (ed.). 1985. *The Hermeneutics Reader: Texts of the German Tradition from the Enlightenment to the Present*. New York: Continuum.

Murrel, Peter. 1983. "Did the Theory of Market Socialism Answer the Challenge of Ludwig von Mises?," *History of Political Economy* 15, no. 1 (Spring).

Muzondo, Timothy R. 1979. "On the Theory of the Competitive Labor-Managed Firm under Price Uncertainty," *Journal of Comparative Economics* 3, no. 2 (June).

———. 1980. "On the Theory of the Competitive Labor-Managed Firm under Price Uncertainty: A Correction and Comment," *Journal of Comparative Economics* 4, no. 3 (September).

Myrick, Herbert. 1895. *How to Cooperate: A Manual for Cooperators*. New York: Orange Judd Co.

Natanson, Maurice (ed.). 1973. *Phenomenology and the Social Sciences*. 2 vols. Evanston: Northwestern University Press.

Neary, Hugh M. 1984. "Labor-Managed Cournot Oligopoly and Industry Output: A Comment," *Journal of Comparative Economics* 8, no. 3 (September).

Nutter, G. Warren. 1983. *Political Economy and Freedom: A Collection of Essays*. Indianapolis: Liberty Press.

O'Driscoll, Gerald P. 1977. *Economics as a Coordination Problem: The Contributions of Friedrich A. Hayek*. Kansas City: Sheed Andrews and McMeel, Inc.

O'Driscoll, Gerald P., and Mario J. Rizzo (1985). *The Economics of Time and Ignorance*. New York: Basil Blackwell.

Offe, Claus. 1984. *Contradictions of the Welfare State*. Cambridge: MIT Press.

Owen, Robert. 1817. *A New View of Society, or Essays on the Formation of the Human Character*. London: Rand A. Taylor.

Pašić, Najdan. 1988. "From Party-State Monolithism to Pluralism of Self-Management Interests," *Socialist Thought and Practice* 28, no. 3-4.

Patinkin, Don. 1965. *Money, Interest and Prices*. New York: Harper and Row.

Patterson, S. Howard. 1929. *Some Aspects of Industry*. New York: McGraw-Hill.

Pejovich, Svetozar. 1966. *The Market-Planned Economy of Yugoslavia*. Minneapolis: University of Minnesota Press.

———. 1973. "The Banking System and the Investment Behavior of the Yugoslav

Firm." In Morris Bornstein (ed.), *Plan and Market: Economic Reform in Eastern Europe* (New Haven: Yale University Press, 1973) pp. 285-311.

————. 1984. "The Incentive to Innovate Under Alternative Property Rights," *Cato Journal* 4, no. 2 (Fall).

————. 1990. "A Property-Rights Analysis of the Yugoslav Miracle," *The Annals* 507 (January).

Perlman, Selig. 1937. *A History of Trade Unionism in the United States*. New York: Macmillan Co.

————. 1949. *A Theory of the Labor Movement*. New York: Augustus M. Kelley.

Perry, Stewart. 1978. *Dirty Work, Clean Jobs, Proud Men*. Berkeley: University of California Press.

Petrović, Gajo. 1967. *Marx in the Mid-Twentieth Century: A Yugoslav Philosopher Considers Karl Marx's Writings*. Garden City, N.Y.: Doubleday and Co.

Petrović, Gajo, and Wolfdietrich Schmied-Kowarzich (eds.). 1985. *Die gegenwartige Bedeu tung des Marxschen Denkens*. Bachum: Germinal Verlag.

Plokker, Karin. 1990. "The Development of Individual and Cooperative Labour Activity in the Soviet Union," *Soviet Studies* 42, no. 3 (July).

Polan, A. J. 1984. *Lenin and the End of Politics*. Berkeley: University of California Press.

Polanyi, Michael. 1951. *The Logic of Liberty*. Chicago: University of Chicago Press.

————. 1957. "The Foolishness of History," *Encounter* 9, no. 5 (November).

————. 1958. *Personal Knowledge: Towards a Post- Critical Philosophy*. Chicago: University of Chicago Press.

————. 1959. *The Study of Man*. Chicago: University of Chicago Press.

Polkinghorne, Donald. 1983. *Methodology for the Human Sciences: Systems of Inquiry*. Albany, N.Y.: State University of New York Press.

Powell, Raymond P. 1977. "Plan Execution and the Workability of Soviet Planning," *Journal of Comparative Economics*. Vol. 1, no. 1 (March). Reprinted in Morris Bornstein (ed.), *The Soviet Economy: Continuity and Change* (Boulder, Colo.: Westview Press, 1981), pp. 39-59.

Prout, Christopher. 1985. *Market Socialism in Yugoslavia*. New York: Oxford University Press.

Prychitko, David. 1987. "Ludwig Lachmann and the Farther Reaches of Austrian Economics," *Critical Review* 1, no. 3 (Summer).

————. 1988. "Marxism and Decentralized Socialism," *Critical Review* 2, no. 4 (Fall).

————. 1990a. "Perestroika in Yugoslavia: Lessons from Four Decades of Self-Management," *Global Economic Policy* 2, no. 2.

————. 1990b. "Socialism as Cartesian Legacy: The Radical Element in F. A. Hayek's *The Fatal Conceit*," *Market Process* 8.

————. 1990c. "Toward an Interpretive Economics: Some Hermeneutical Issues," *Methodus* 2, no. 2 (December).

————. 1990d. "The Welfare State: What is Left?," *Critical Review* 4, no. 4 (Fall).

Pryor, Frederic L. 1983. "The Economics of Production Co-operatives: A Reader's Guide," *Annals of Public and Cooperative Economy* 54, no. 2 (April-June).

Putterman, Louis. 1980. "Voluntary Collectivization: A Model of Producers' Institutional Choice," *Journal of Comparative Economics* 4, no. 2 (June).

———. 1984. "On Some Recent Explanations of Why Capital Hires Labor," *Economic Inquiry* 22 (April).

Rabinow, Paul, and William M. Sullivan (eds.). 1979. *Interpretive Social Science: A Reader*. Los Angeles: University of California Press.

Reibel, R. 1975. "The Workingman's Production Association or the Republic in the Workshop." In Vanek (ed.) (1975), pp. 39-46.

Remington, Thomas F. 1984. *Building Socialism in Bolshevik Russia: Ideology and Industrial Organization, 1917-1921*. Pittsburgh: University of Pittsburgh Press.

Richardson, G. B. 1959. "Equilibrium, Expectations, and Information," *Economic Journal* 69 (June).

Ricoeur, Paul. 1976. *Interpretation Theory: Discourse and the Surplus of Meaning*. Fort Worth: University of Texas Press.

Rizzo, Mario J. (ed.). 1979. *Time, Uncertainty and Disequilibrium*. Lexington, Mass.: Lexington Books.

Robbins, Lionel. 1934. *The Great Depression*. New York: Macmillan.

Roberts, Paul Craig. 1971. *Alienation and the Soviet Economy: Toward a General Theory of Marxian Alienation, Organizational Principles, and the Soviet Economy*. Albuquerque: University of New Mexico Press.

Roberts, Paul Craig, and Matthew A. Stephenson. 1973. *Marx's Theory of Exchange, Alienation, and Crisis*. Stanford: Hoover Institution Press.

Rothbard, Murray N. 1970. *Power and Market: Government and the Economy*. Menlo Park, Calif.: Institute for Humane Studies, Inc.

Rothschild, Joyce, and J. Allen Whitt. 1986. *The Cooperative Workplace: Potentials and Dilemmas of Organizational Democracy and Participation*. New York: Cambridge University Press.

Rus, Veljko. 1986. "Private and Public Ownership in Yugoslavia," *Scandinavian Journal of Management Studies* (May).

Rus, Velko, et al. 1977. "Participative Decision-Making under Conditions of Uncertainty," paper presented at the Second International Conference on Participation, Workers' Control, and Self-Management" (Paris).

Rutland, Peter. 1985. *The Myth of the Plan: Lessons from the Soviet Planning Experience*. La Salle, Ill.: Open Court.

Sacks, Stephen. 1973. *Entry of New Competitors in Yugoslav Market Socialism*. Berkeley: Institute of International Studies.

Saltman, Richard B. 1983. *The Social and Political Thought of Michael Bakunin*. Westport, Conn.: Greenwood Press.

Samuels, Warren J. (ed.). 1980. *The Methodology of Economic Thought*. New Brunswick, N.J.: Transaction.

Schrenk, Martin, Cyrus Ardalan, and N.A. El Tatawy. 1979. *Yugoslavia: Self-management Socialism and the Challenges of Development*. Baltimore: Johns Hopkins University Press.

Schumpeter, Joseph A. 1954. *History of Economic Analysis*. New York: Oxford University Press.

———. 1976. *Capitalism, Socialism and Democracy*. New York: Harper and Row.

Selucký, Radoslav. 1979. *Marxism, Socialism, Freedom: Towards a General Democratic Theory of Labour-Managed Systems*. New York: St. Martin's Press.

Sen, Amartya K. 1966. "Labour Allocation in a Cooperative Enterprise," *Review of Economic Studies* 33.

Sexton, Richard J. 1986. "The Formation of Cooperatives: A Game-Theoretic Approach with Implications for Cooperative Finance, Decision Making, and Stability," *American Journal of Agricultural Economics* 68, no. 2 (May).

Shafritz, Jay M., and J. Steven Ott. 1987. *Classics of Organization Theory*. Chicago: The Dorsey Press.

Shavell, S. 1979. "Risk Sharing and Incentives in the Principal Agent Relationship," *Bell Journal of Economics*. Vol. 10, no. 1 (Spring).

Shaw, Albert. 1886. "Cooperation in a Western City," *Publications of the American Economic Association* 1, no. 4 (September).

———. 1888. "Cooperation in Minnesota," *History of Cooperation in the United States*. Studies in Historical and Political Science. Sixth Series, no. 4-6. Baltimore: Johns Hopkins University.

Sher, Gerson S. (ed.). 1978. *Marxist Humanism and Praxis*. Buffalo, N.Y.: Prometheus Books.

Shirom, Arie. 1972. "The Industrial Relations System of Industrial Cooperatives in the United States, 1880-1935," *Labor History* 13, no. 4 (Fall).

Simić, Miodrag, and Aleksandar Žikić. 1987. *Yugoslav Chamber of Economy in the National Economic System: The Law of Affiliation in the Yugoslav Chamber of Economy and the Statute of the Chamber With Commentary*. Belgrade: Export Press.

Sirc, Ljubo. 1979. *The Yugoslav Economy Under Self-Management*. London: Macmillan.

Sismonde, J. C. L. Simonde de. 1991. *New Principles of Political Economy*. Trans. and annotated by Richard Hyse. New Brunswick: Transaction.

Sohn-Rethel, Alfred. 1978. *Intellectual and Manual Labor: A Critique of Epistemology*. Atlantic Highlands, N.J.: Humanities Press.

Staatz, J. M. 1983. "The Cooperative as a Coalition: A Game Theoretic Approach," *American Journal of Agricultural Economics*. Vol. 65, no. 5 (December).

Stanić, S. 1980. "Ownership." In Bogdan Trifunovic (ed.), *A Handbook of Yugoslav Socialist Self-Management* (Belgrade: Socialist Thought and Practice, 1980), pp. 177-86.

Steinherr, Alfred, and J. F. Thisse. 1979a. "Are Labor- Managers Really Perverse?," *Economic Letters* 2.

———. 1979b. "Is There a Negatively-Sloped Supply Curve in the Labour-Managed Firm?," *Economic Analysis and Workers' Management* 13, no. 1-2.

Stephen, Frank H. 1984. *The Economic Analysis of Producers' Cooperatives*. New York: St. Martin's Press.

Stojanović, Svetozar. 1981. *In Search of Democracy in Socialism: History and Party Consciousness*. Buffalo, N.Y.: Prometheus.

———. 1988. *Perestroika: From Marxism and Bolshevism to Gorbachev*. Buffalo, N.Y.: Prometheus.

Supek, Rudi. 1971. "Some Contradictions and Insufficiencies of Yugoslav Self-Managing Socialism," *Praxis* 7. Reprinted in Marković and Petrović (1979), pp. 249-71.

———. 1989. "P. J. Proudhon and Two Notions of Self-Management," paper presented at the conference "Anarchism: Community and Utopia" (Dubrovnik: Inter-University Center for postgraduate studies, March 20-31, 1989).

Šuvar, Stipe. 1988. "Let Socialism Start Moving Forward Again to a Better Future," *Socialist Thought and Practice* 28, no. 7-10.

Sweezy, Paul. 1964. "The Transition from Socialism to Capitalism," *Monthly Review*.

Sweezy, Paul M. (ed.). 1975. *Karl Marx and the Close of his System and Boehm-Bawerk's Criticism of Marx*. Clifton, N.J.: Augustus M. Kelley.

Taub, Alan J. 1974. "The Cooperative Firm Under Uncertainty," *Eastern Economic Journal* 1, no. 2 (April).

Taylor, Fred M. 1929. "The Guidance of Production in a Socialist State." In Lippincott (ed.) (1964), pp. 39-54.

Taylor, Frederick Winslow. 1916. "The Principles of Scientific Management," *Bulletin of the Taylor Society* (December). Reprinted in Shafritz and Ott (1987), pp. 66-81.

Temkin, Gabriel. 1989. "On Economic Reforms in Socialist Countries: The Debate on Economic Calculation under Socialism Revisited," *Communist Economies* 1, no. 1.

Thomas, Henk, and Chris Logan. 1982. *Mondragon: An Economic Analysis*. Reading, Mass.: Allen and Unwin.

Towne, Henry R. 1886. "The Engineer as Economist," *Transactions of the American Society of Mechanical Engineers*, vol. 7. Reprinted in Shafritz and Ott (1987), pp. 47–51.

Traub, Rainer. 1978. "Lenin and Taylor: The Fate of 'Scientific-Management' in the (Early) Soviet Union," *Telos* no. 37 (Fall).

Truzzi, Marcello (ed.). 1974. *Verstehen: Subjective Understanding in the Social Sciences*. Reading, Mass.: Addison Wesley.

Tyson, Laura D'Andrea. 1980. *The Yugoslav Economic System and its Performance in the 1970s*. Berkeley: Institute of International Studies.

U.S. Bureau of Labor. 1898. *Annual Report of the Commissioner of Labor: Hand and Machine Labor*. 2 vols. Washington, DC: U.S. Bureau of Labor.

Vanek, Jaroslav. 1970. *The General Theory of Labor-Managed Market Economies*. Ithaca, N.Y.: Cornell University Press.

———. 1971a. "The Basic Theory of Financing Participatory Firms," Working Paper no. 27, Department of Economics, Cornell University. Reprinted in Vanek (ed.) (1975), pp. 445-55.

———. 1971b. *The Participatory Economy: An Evolutionary Hypothesis and a Strategy for Development*. Ithaca, N.Y.: Cornell University Press.

———. (ed.). 1975. *Self-Management: Economic Liberation of Man*. Baltimore: Penguin Books.

———. 1977. *The Labor-Managed Economy*. Ithaca, N.Y.: Cornell University Press.

———. 1988. "Vienna Conference 1988—Opening Discussion." Presented at the Fifth International Conference on the Economics of Self-Management (Vienna, July 6-8).

Vaughn, Karen I. 1980a. "Does it Matter that Costs are Subjective?", *Southern Journal of Economics* 46, no. 3 (January).

————. 1980b. "Economic Calculation under Socialism: The Austrian Contribution," *Economic Inquiry* 18 (October).

Virtue, G. O. 1905. "The Cooperative Coopers of Minneapolis," *Quarterly Journal of Economics* 19, no. 3 (August).

————. 1932. "The End of the Cooperative Coopers," *Quarterly Journal of Economics* 46, no. 3 (May).

Vranicki, Pedrag. 1965. "Socialism and the Problem of Alienation." In Fromm (ed.) (1965), pp. 299-313.

Walicki, Andrzey. 1988. "Karl Marx as Philosopher of Freedom," *Critical Review* 2, no. 4 (Fall).

Walker, Francis A. 1892. *Political Economy*. New York: Holt and Co.

————. 1968. *The Wages Question: A Treatise on Wages and the Wages Class*. New York: Augustus M. Kelley.

Wallimann, Isidor. 1981. *Estrangement: Marx's Conception of Human Nature and the Division of Labor*. Westport, Conn.: Greenwood Press.

Walsh, George E. 1905. "The Life of a Barrel," *Scientific American*. (January 21, 1905), p. 39.

Ward, Benjamin N. 1958. "The Firm in Illyria: Market Syndicalism," *American Economic Review* 48, no. 4 (September).

————. 1967. "Marxism-Horvatism: A Yugoslav Theory of Socialism," *American Economic Review* 57, no. 3 (June).

Ware, Norman J. 1959. *The Labor Movement in the United States, 1860–1895: A Study in Democracy*. Gloucester, Mass.: Peter Smith.

Watkins, Gordon S. 1922. *An Introduction to the Study of Labor Problems*. New York: Thomas Y. Crowell Co.

Weber, Max. 1978. *Economy and Society: An Outline of Interpretive Sociology*. Berkeley: University of California Press.

Weinstein, James. 1968. *The Corporate Ideal in the Liberal State, 1900–1918*. Boston: Beacon Press.

Whyte, William Foote, and Kathleen King Whyte. 1988. *Making Mondragon: The Growth and Dynamics of the Worker Cooperative Complex*. Ithaca N.Y.: ILR Press.

Wieser, Friedrich von. 1967. *Social Economics*. New York: Augustus M. Kelley.

Williamson, Oliver E. 1975. *Markets and Hierarchies: Analysis and Anti-trust Implications*. New York: Free Press.

Woo, Henry K. H. 1986. *What's Wrong with Formalization in Economics? An Epistemological Critique*. Newark, Calif.: Victoria Press.

Wright, Carrol D. 1887. "An Historical Sketch of the Knights of Labor," *Quarterly Journal of Economics* 1 (January).

Zaleski, Eugene. 1980. *Stalinist Planning for Economic Growth*. London: Macmillan.

Zerzan, John. 1984. "Taylorism and Unionism: The Origins of a Partnership," *Telos* no. 60 (Summer).

Index

of, 108; use of machinery within,
109, 110, 116 n.21
—Excelsior Cooperative Barrel Co.,
107
—Hennepin County Barrel Co., 107,
108, 110, 111, 112, 116 nn.19, 21
—Liberty Barrel Co., 107
—North Star Barrel Co.: assets of,
108, 112; as joint stock company,
116 n.24; membership of, 107; 108,
110, 111, 112, 115 n.15; merger with
Cooperative Manufacturing Barrel
Co., 112; origin of, 107; output of,
108; use of machinery within, 109,
110, 116 n.21
—Northwestern Barrel Co., 108, 109
—Phoenix Barrel Co., 107
Cooperation: appropriated by Taylorism, 38; change of meaning concerning, 37, 56 n.14; classical economists
on, 33–37, 54, 55 nn.2, 3, 6, 56
nn.13, 14; Marx on, 7–10; 10 n.4; as
method to replace strikes, 105;
"partial," 105; utopian socialists'
views on, 1–5, 10 n.1
Cooperative movement, 2, 7; American, 26, 101, 102, 104–5; British,
102; classical economists' discussion
of, 33–37, 55 nn.1, 3; French, 34; in
nineteenth-century socialism, 1–10;
role of religion in, 36, 56 n.10
Cooperatives, consumers', 7, 33, 55
n.6
Cooperatives, producers', 34, 35, 36,
37; boom of in America, 104–5;
classical economists on, 33–37, 54,
103, 113 n.1; decline of interest in,
40; degenerating into joint stock
companies, 7, 36, 102; goal of, 1;
"inherent weakness" questioned,
102, 113; Marx's view of, 7–8, 21;
and monitoring problem, 120–21
n.1; motivations of, 2, 36, 56 n.12;
in Paris Commune, 8; problem of
judging success among, 103–4, 112–
13; reasons for failure, 36; and Taylorism, 38; viability in market system, 84, 101–13, 118–20 (see also

Cooperage cooperatives); virtues,
118–19
Coopers Monthly Journal (trade journal), 115 n.18
Cooper's Union, 107, 111–12
Coordination: intertemporal, 89; in la-
bor-managed economy, 78 n.3;
through "trial and error," 42
Coordination, *ex ante*, 40–41, 54, 78
n.4, 83–86, 88, 90, 118–19; as al-
leged technical problem, 86, 87;
among BOALs, 92–93, 94–96; as
"essence of planning," 83. *See also*
Planning
Coordination, *ex post*, 40, 79 n.7, 85,
88–90. *See also* Competition; Mar-
ket Process
Cowen, Tyler, 81 n.26
Coyne, Franklin E., 109, 115–16 n.18
Credit, 4, 20
Crisis, Marxian theory of, 18, 29 n.11,
59 n.34
*Critique of Hegel's "Philosophy of
Right"* (Marx), 22
Critique of the Gotha Program (Marx),
10 n.4
Curtis, Chauncey W., 105, 106, 107,
114 nn.5, 7

De-alienation. *See* Alienation; Free-
dom, in Marx's view; Praxis
Decentralization, xii, xiii, xiv, 4, 24,
27, 33, 51, 52, 53–54, 59 n.35, 63,
84, 91–94, 95, 99 n.18, 117
Democracy and Socialism (Kardelj),
95
Democratic centralism, 66
Demsetz, Harold, on monitoring prob-
lem, 120–21 n.1
Descartes, Rene, 82 n.28
Description of Industry (Adams), 56
n.14
Despotism: of capitalist boss, 7, 14,
15, 18; of central planning board,
25, 27; of revolutionary minority, 5.
See also Totalitarian problem
Dialectical materialism, 30 n.15

also Centralization; Totalitarian
problem
La theorie des quatres mouvements
(Fourier), 2
Thomas, Henk, 104
Time preference and ownership, 71–
72, 80 n.17
Totalitarianism, xi, 49–51; anticipated
by Bakunin, 6; as bastardized Marxism, xv; compared to self-managed
socialist ideal, 63. *See also* Statism
Totalitarian problem, 45–47, 49–51,
53, 55, 58–59 n.31, 59 n.33; in Yugoslavia, 93–96, 99–100 n.22, 100
nn.24, 25 (*see also* Socialism, Yugoslav)
Towne, Henry R., 37
Transition period, 59; Cole's view of,
52–53; disagreement over, 79 n.8; as
logically distinct from fully-evolved
socialism, 30 n.14; Marx's utopian
approach to, 60 n.36; totalitarian
problem and, 48–49
Twenty-first Annual Cooperative Congress, 35
Tyson, Laura D'Andrea, on tension in
Yugoslav self-management, 100 n.25

Unions, acceptance of scientific management by, 57 n.18
Universal suffrage; in Marx's critique
of Hegel, 23–24; in Paris Commune,
8
Use value, 17

Vanek, Jaroslav, 71, 80 n.16, 99 n.20;
general model of, 63–64, 77 n.1, 77–
78 n.3; on investment, 72–73; on
limits of neoclassical model, 76, 81–
82 n.27; model distinguished from
Horvat's, 78 n.4, 96–97 n.1; on supportive structure, 97 n.1
Vaughn, Karen I.: on misunderstanding in socialist calculation debate,
44–45; on subjective element of
cost, 98 n.11

Virtue, G.O., on cooperage cooperatives, 110, 111, 115 n.17, 116 nn.19,
24
Vranicki, Pedrag, xvii n.4, 49

The Wages Question (Walker), 35
Walicki, Andrzey, xvii n.3
Walker, Francis A., 35, 36, 55 n.4, 80
n.14
Wallimann, Isidor, 29 n.7
Walras, Leon, 44, 58 n.30, 74
Walsh, George E., 111
War Communism, 45
Ward, Benjamin N., 71, 74; on insta-
bility of self-managed firm, 67–69,
79 nn.10, 11, 12, 13, 80 n.14; on
"open mindedness" in economic
theory, 73
Ware, Norman J., 114 n.4
War planning in Germany, 38–39
Watkins, Gordon S., 116 n.24
Weber, Max, 57 n.24
Welfare state, 29 n.11, 37, 59 n.34
Whitt, J. Allen, 10 n.2, 56 n.12
Whyte, Kathleen King, 104
Whyte, William Foote, 104
Wieser, Friedrich von, on knowledge
problem, 57 n.25
Williamson, Oliver E., 120 n.1
Workers' council: conflicts of interest
and, 94; work units and, 65. *See
also* BOAL; Self-managed enter-
prise
Workers' self-management. *See* Social-
ism, Self-managed

Young Hegelians, 5
Yugoslav Chamber of Economy, as
organ of state power, 94–95
Yugoslavia. *See* Socialism, Yugoslav

Zerzan, John, 57 n.18
Žikić, Aleksandar, on tension in Yugoslav socialism, 94–95

ABOUT THE AUTHOR

DAVID L. PRYCHITKO is Associate Professor in the Department of Economics at the State University of New York at Oswego. He specializes in political economy and comparative systems studies and has written articles for *Critical Review*, *Global Economic Policy*, and *Methodus*.